To Jerry and Carmen,

We give you a piece of the west to remind you of us. Thank you for your hospitality, your friendship, your kindness, and your love. Every time we get together, we just pick up where we left off!

With Our Love,
Steve and Barbara
August 1994

CROUTONS on a COW·PIE
VOLUME II

Cowboy Poetry By

Baxter Black

illustrated by

***Bob Black,
Don Gill,
Dave Holl &
Charlie Marsh***

COYOTE COWBOY COMPANY
RECORD STOCKMAN PRESS

DENVER   1992

All poems written by Baxter Black

Copyright © 1992 by Baxter Black

Published by   Coyote Cowboy Company
Record Stockman Press
4800 Wadsworth Blvd.
Wheat Ridge, Colorado 80033
All rights reserved.

Cover design by Salamander Graphics

LIBRARY OF CONGRESS CATALOGING IN PUBLICATION DATA
Main entry under:
Cowboy Poetry

Bibliography: p
1. Coyote Cowboy Poetry
2. Cowboys - Poetry
3. Poetry - Cowboy
4. Humor - Cowboy
5. Agriculture - Poetic Comment

I. Black, Baxter, 1945-

Library of Congress #88-71575
ISBN 0-939343-12-6

OTHER BOOKS BY BAXTER
* THE COWBOY AND HIS DOG © 1980
* A RIDER, A ROPER AND A HECK'UVA WINDMILL MAN © 1982
ON THE EDGE OF COMMON SENSE, THE BEST SO FAR © 1983
* DOC, WHILE YER HERE © 1984
BUCKAROO HISTORY © 1985
COYOTE COWBOY POETRY © 1986
✔ CROUTONS ON A COW PIE © 1988
✔ THE BUCKSKIN MARE © 1989
✔ COWBOY STANDARD TIME © 1990

* *Included entirely in Coyote Cowboy Poetry 1986*
✔ *Included entirely in Croutons On A Cow Pie, Vol II 1992*

FOREWORD

In the fall of 1970 my version of the American dream came true. I found a sizeable chunk of high desert country even we could afford. Years of drawing cowboy wages did not leave much of a nest egg but I was blessed with three small children who believed I could do anything and a wife who kept her opinions to herself. I latched onto this "affordable starter outfit" like a pit bull with an overbite.

The first year was a mite shaky; the bred ewes I bought dropped lambs with white muscle disease, spring wind electrocuted the barley crop and in July the drought came back.

By 1980, the homely looking outfit had made good hands out of all three kids, had their mother working in town for grocery money, and had me studying agriculture real hard. I subscribed to every farm and ranch publication I could think of and pored over each one looking for alternative crops, alternative irrigation systems, alternative anything.

One of the publications was THE RECORD STOCKMAN and in among the semi-relevant advice articles from various extension experts, old cowboy obituaries, market reports, and bureaucratic prognostications, were the musings of a fledgling, one newspaper columnist named Baxter Black.

All that remains of my intensive research project (carefully smoothed into a shoe box and stored in my closet) are a few Ace Reid cartoons, most of Baxter's early columns, and a quote I ran across from Aristotle that said, "Agriculture is a cooperative not a creative effort", that made me wonder if I was cooperating hard enough.

It is fair enough, I suppose, to ask why I discarded all that expensive advice and kept the poems and often tongue in cheek columns of a self-proclaimed sorry team roper and general misfit.

The answer to that complicated question is simple enough, I kept the stuff I needed most. Baxter's poems are using poems and comparing them to academic poetry (written for purposes of tenure) is like comparing the horses you'll find on a cow outfit with the pampered, non-productive darlings you'll find over fed and under used in a stall in suburban Baltimore.

We, those of us who struggle to earn a living in a business whose return to risk and management might make the sternest investment counselor collapse in a fit of giggles, are Baxter Black's subjects and his greatest fans.

His poems ring true because he knows us well enough to never pull his punches.

If you have the opportunity to attend one of his packed house performances and can generate the discipline to watch the crowd instead of Baxter, you will see ranch wives laughing and looking fondly sideways at their mates as if to say, "Yes, that's just the way this old fool acts."

Baxter's poems tell us he knows us well and loves us anyway. He has an uncanny ability to mix laughter and tears in just the right proportion so we know he knows and returns the love a thousand fold.

If you buy this book (and you should) and read it (and you should) and cannot find anything to laugh at or cry at but still want to venture west and investigate a cowboy, I would recommend you stay on paved roads.

Vess Quinlan
Colorado rancher, scholar and poet

TABLE OF CONTENTS

TABLE OF CONTENTS (continued)

With special thanks to
Sheryl Suhr, friend and secretary;
Harry Green, Dan Green
and the Record Stockman . . .

. . . and dedicated to Ace Reid.
When it came to tellin' cowboy stories,
he's the best I ever saw.

DRESSIN' UP

Dressin' up to certain good folks
Might mean a suit and a tie
Designer socks, a diamond ring
Or hair like the fourth of July!

But out where we make a livin'
Tennis shoes don't fit the bill.
They don't set too good in a stirrup,
I reckon they never will.

We're more into spurs, hats and leggin's
'Cause punchin' cows ain't all romance
But cowboys clean up on occasion
For weddings, a funeral or dance.

The dress code for everyday cowboys
Ain't changed since Grandpa got wise,
A good pair of boots, yer Sunday hat
And yer newest pair of levi's.

Besides, deckin' a cowboy out
In street shoes, a suit and a tie
Would make as good an impression
As croutons on a cow pie.

COUP DE GRACE

"Well, at least it isn't broken," *he said as he wiped his face*
  With his good arm. "Although it might be a smidgen outta place.
That sucker sure did buck hard! I'm glad I was wearin' my hat
  Or I'da punched right through that net wire fence and hung there like a bat!

Dadgummit! Where's the rest of my shirt? All but the sleeves are gone!
  And my chest has got a pattern you could make a waffle on!
I remember him a'squallin' with my collar in his teeth
  As I flopped from neck to shoulder like a rubber Christmas wreath!

Have ya seen my other batwing leg? I had it, I'da sworn.
  I never wear just half a pair. Musta hooked it on the horn
When he ran it up my pantleg where my inseam used to be!
  And my off hind boot is missin'! Aw, hell, that don't bother me,

It could still be in the stirrup 'cause I had a deadman's grip!
  I made several revolutions from his belly to his hip,
Checked the bosal and the backcinch as I orbited around!
  He pumped me like a plumber plungin' dirty water down!

Then bounced me off the buckin' rolls when he went to changin' gears!
  I did a back flip and catapulted out between his ears
But I hung tight to the neck rein as I spun and ricocheted
  Like someone tied a chicken to a helicopter blade!

I was airborne several minutes 'fore I landed in a heap
  And, exceptin' for this hatband there ain't nothin' left to keep!
Can't remember if he kicked me but these tracks are livin' proof,
  This here trademark on my pocket looks suspiciously like hoof.

Don't know how the sucker bucked me off. It happened way too fast
  But nobody has to tell this fool that I been coop de grassed!
It's a story old as cowboys and sometimes the horses win
  But, at least it isn't broken, so best catch'im up again."

LOST

A source of pride amongest cowboys
　Is knowin' the lay of the land
And any poor fool that gets lost
　They figger ain't much of a hand!

　　They said, "We'll meet up at Bull Crick!"
　　　Then looked at me like a trainee!
　　"Draw me a map and I'll find it!
　　　Columbus had nothin' on me!"

Daylight broke into my windshield,
　Headed south and loaded for bear.
I turned at the Grasmere station.
　I should'a shot myself right there!

　　Nothin' was like they described it,
　　　No mailbox where it should be,
　　No coyote hide on a fence post,
　　　Now where's Mary's Crick s'posed to be?

Their map showed tourist attractions
　Including, I swear, Noah's Ark!
Little ol' tricklin' Sheep Crick
　Was wider than Yellowstone Park!

　　I crossed the Cow and the Horse Crick
　　　And cricks named for Nickles and Dimes,
　　Through Nit Crick, Louse Crick and Crab Crick!
　　　Crossed Willer Crick twenty-eight times!

I drove demented and crazy!
　A'chasin' my tail like a dog!
Coursing through desert and mountain,
　Brush thicket and cattail bog,

Fighting back panic, I'm thinkin',
  'I could die and never be found!
Worse yet, I'll look like a gunsel
  Who can't find his way outta town!'

    Harold was boss of the truckers.
      I figgered he might set me right.
    So, I called him up on the two-way
      And explained my desperate plight.

He said, "Describe yer surroundings."
  I looked for a landmark somewhere,
"Ain't nothin' but rocks and sagebrush!"
  He said, "Sonny, yer almost there!"

THE SALES CALL

Ranch women have a lot in common with prisoners in solitary confinement. They are often starved for conversation. This isn't meant to be a reflection on their husbands, if they have one, 'cause he spends all day talkin' to the dog, his horse, stray cows, passing motorists and itinerant mammals and it kinda depletes his normally plentiful wit. By the time he comes in for supper all he can do is grunt and fall asleep in the Barcalounger.

So when a stranger shows up at the ranch, he's usually welcome company. Which is why there is a grain of truth in the old jokes that begins, "Did you hear the one about the farmer's wife and the traveling salesman?"

Hilda found herself visiting at Molly's ranch home one afternoon. It was a visit that had to be planned since Molly lived forty miles from town. Just as they were pouring the second cup, they heard a knock on the door. Molly answered. She was nearly bowled over by a frayed looking man pulling a vacuum cleaner behind him like a gut shot varmint draggin' his entrails!

He spoke with the conviction of an evangelist down to his last parishioner!

Molly started to say something but he raised a hand in protest, *"Afternoon, ladies, dee-lighted to catch all of you home! Was just passin' through and saw your cars in the drive. Beautiful home, by the way I see you collect antique kerosene lanterns... This is your lucky day... both of you!*

"I happen to represent Takum & Run, Chicago, Illinois, manufacturers of the finest vacuum cleaners in the free world today! The Suckitup Two with power nozzle and self-cleaning dander attachment... nice wood stove, there... for hard to pet dogs..."

He talked without letup for 45 minutes while the ladies sat amazed at his stamina. They drew back in astonishment when he upended a plastic feed sack on Molly's shag carpet! Steel balls, charcoal briquets, chicken bones, sawdust, fingernail clippings, volcanic ash and soybean meal cascaded into a pile!

He spread it across the carpet with a sweep of his hand, *"And to prove everything I said is the gospel truth, if this vacuum cleaner doesn't pick up every speck of this mess I've made, I'll get down on my hands and knees and lick it up myself!"*

Molly leaned forward, "You better git out yer chapstick, Sonny, I ain't got no 'lectricity!"

COWBOY HEAVEN

I never did do it for the money
I guess you done figgered that out
But I's never broke, fer long anyways
Gettin' rich ain't what it's about

> Gettin' high on the smell of a sunrise
> A'horseback a long way from camp
> Or the sound of the crickets competin'
> With a hissin' kerosene lamp

That's reason enough to be out here, that
And livin' my life nearly free
'Cause I ain't punchin' cows fer the payday
It means more than money to me

> If I could I'd stay out here forever
> Without meanin' no disrespect
> To them folks sellin' box seats in Glory
> And passin' the plate to collect

Somewhere inside me they say there's a soul
Just waitin' to fly when I croak
And I'd sure be a bit disappointed
If Heaven was only a joke

> And I'm ready to go, if I have to
> Though I plan on wearin' my hat
> But I hope it's as good as they claim it
> 'Cause it's hard to beat where I'm at

Some believers have reached the conclusion
That men get recycled like cans
And eventually wind up in Heaven
After wearin' numerous brands

> If that's true, then my soul prob'ly lit here
> By chance, on a wing and a prayer
> Which explains why it's so much like Heaven
> 'Cause maybe I'm already there

SATURDAY NIGHT

Dang it, someone spilt their coffee on the deck of cards again.
  Prob'ly one of the new guys. This place looks like a den
  Of hibernatin' coyotes. Hell, they've broke the other chair!
  And I'd been countin' on a little game of solitaire.

Kids. I've seen a million comin' through that bunkhouse door.
  They blow through here like tumbleweeds, I've give up keepin' score.
  Tonight they're down at Mona's no doubt spendin' their last dime
  'Cause we pull out on Monday. But way back there was a time

I'd been right in amongst'em but I quit goin' to town.
  I got a box for pop cans but they're scattered all around!
  It doesn't seem too much to ask to keep the trash picked up.
  Matilda whelped another batch. Romero took a pup

To train it. That's okay, but the corner by his bed
  Is littered with old papers. So he could learn to read, he said.
  Pretty funny, that Romero. Now's where's my Gel-U-Sel?
  I could work on that macardie I was braidin'. What the hell,

I might just go to Mona's. Show them kids a thing or two.
  They think I'm old and grouchy but if they only knew
  I'm just tired of playin' wet nurse to a string of buckaroos
  Who live to ride and rollick, but until they've paid their dues

They won't get the satisfaction of seein' me impressed
  By their endless balface windys or stirrin' up the nest.
  They can learn by my example. Maybe even save a buck.
  And I would go down to Mona's but I lent the lads my truck.

COWBOY TIME

If Genesis was right on track concerning Adam's birth
And seven days was all it took to build the planet Earth,

Then where does carbon dating fit? And all the dinosaurs?
Plus all that other ancient stuff that happened on our shores?

Now, I believe in scientists. They aren't just lunatics!
But I believe in Genesis, which leaves me in a fix.

The answer finally came to me while making up this rhyme,
God made the earth in seven days, but...that was Cowboy Time!

Have you ever called the shoer to set aside a day?
You scrutinize your calendar, say, "Tuesday'd be okay."

The big day comes, you take off work, alas, he's never seen.
You call him back and he inquires, "Which Tuesday did you mean?"

Did you ever place an order to get a saddle made?
An A-Fork tree and padded seat with silver hand-inlaid.

As decades pass, all you can do is sit around and eat
So by the time it finally comes you've padded your own seat!

A friend came by on July 4th. He swore he couldn't stay
But then he said, "For just a bit." He left on Christmas day!

'Soon,' to all my cowboy friends means next year...or tomorrow
Depending whether in the deal he plans to lend or borrow!

'A couple days,' 'a little while,' 'not long,' or 'right away!'
Should not be taken li'trally in cowboyville today.

But like I said, the precedent was set so long ago.
The angels had to learn themselves what all good cowboys know.

They worried if they didn't work to keep the schedule tight
That Earth would not be finished by the deadline Sunday night.

They'd never learned to think in terms of 'rollin' with the flow'
But God does things on Cowboy Time...to watch the flowers grow.

He bade the angels to relax and said, "For Heaven's sakes,
I'll get it done in seven days...however long it takes!"

THE LONG WAY HOME

The light shined through the swingin' doors
And spilled itself into the street.
It stubbed its toe on a shadow
And fell at the cowboy's feet

Who was part inebriated.
Well, really, . . . substantially blitzed!
He listed to port and swayed like
His momentum was on the fritz!

He scanned the customer parking
In search of his faithful old bay.
Lo and behold there was his horse
But facin' the basakwards way!

"Great Scott! My equine's been damaged!
Tampered with!" the cowboy said.
Then reached the brilliant conclusion
That somebody'd cut off his head!

He rode ol' bay back to the ranch
Without even takin' a breath
With his finger in the windpipe
To keep him from bleedin' to death!

A HUNDRED YEARS TOO LATE

I psychoanalyzed myself
And pondered at my fate.
And realized that I was born
A hundred years too late.

A cowpoke in this day and age
Must learn to specialize.
The fact I'm barely gettin' by
Should come as no surprise.

There was a time when you could tell
A top hand by his hat.
But knowin' cows is not enough,
Geneticists do that!

Once, every puncher worth his salt
Could rope a wild steer.
Now motel cowboys do that trick
At Cheyenne every year.

I might have been a bunkhouse bard
A hundred years ago,
But modern cowboy poets star
On Johnny Carson's show.

Somehow I think if I had lived
When horses reigned supreme
I'd carved my niche in history,
At least that's what I dream.

I'd built my reputation with
Each buckin' bronc I spurred.
My daring exploits would have made
My name a household word.

Amongst the cowboys of today
I'm just an average Joe.
I could have made more of myself
A hundred years ago.

If only fortune would have smiled
And laid my egg back then,
I'd been a bigger fish, for sure,
Instead of ridin' pens.

But I guess I should be thankful
In spite of what I've said.
If I'd been born that long ago
Then right now I'd be dead!

THE ACCIDENT

My ol' friend Wayne had an accident
Seems he'd treated himself to a nip
And came home late with the bottle stashed
In the pocket there on his right hip.

He fumbled around for the house key
'Cause his wife habitually locked it,
Pushed open the door, slipped on the rug
And the bottle broke in his pocket!

He bit his tongue to stifle a scream!
He could feel the pieces of glass
As they cut through his pants and underwear
Carving X's and O's on his *

He raced to the bathroom to check it
And proceeded to make his repairs,
Depleting the entire first aid kit.
Then he quietly slipped up the stairs.

Next morning he slept like a baby
'Til his wife, who was loud as Big Ben,
Shattered his peaceful dreams by saying,
"So, you came home last night . . . drunk again!"

"But, Dear, I . . . I thought you were sleeping?"
*"Yes, I was, but it's perfectly clear,
I just came up from the downstairs throne
And there's band aids all over the mirror!"*

TRIGGERNOMETRY

The 60 seconds that changed my life.

I suspect everybody has one. A chance meeting, a tragedy, a windfall, a lucky ride, a forgiveness, a walk down the aisle. Saul got his on the road to Damascus. Freckles Brown got his on Tornado, Nixon got his when the tape shredder broke and I got mine in a classroom in the spring of 1965.

I had started college majoring in Animal Husbandry. I enjoyed two good years judging livestock, rodeoing, playing music and studying the science of agriculture. The summer of '64 I got antsy and decided to take a shot at veterinary school. This required that I take some courses that I normally would have avoided like a house cat avoids Co-op dog food!

Looming ahead of me were two semesters of Physics and one five hour course of Calculus and Trigonometry. I felt like Gutzon Borglum standing in front of Mt. Rushmore with a garden trowel!

I put off the dreaded math course and dove head first into the Chemistry and Physics. Unfortunately, the pool was drained! The only people who didn't seem to mind my difficulty was the local draft board. To hedge my odds I visited the Navy recruiter. He gave me a test and a physical. I postponed his invitation.

By the second semester I was sinking like a set of car keys. I had squeaked by so far and applied to vet school. I was now taking Chemistry, Physics and the math course intended for Albert Einstein!

In February the Navy checked me again. By March I had a 54 average in math (passing was 60). By April I received the letter from vet school. I had been accepted! Providing that I completed the required courses. I started going to math class like a born again Algebra teacher! Monday through Friday plus a four hour review every Saturday. It was like getting your prostate examined six days a week!

The day final grades were posted I checked Chemistry...a C, Physics...a D, math...Flunked it flatter'n hammered tin foil! The Saturday review teacher's assistant was in her office. I stood in line to talk to her. The student in front of me was complaining about his grade. He'd gotten a B! When my turn came I fell to my knees in front of the harried graduate student. I can still see her...worn sandals, a chipped toenail, flaky skin on her shins, a peasant dress, straight hair and John Denver glasses. I looked up her nostrils and she said, "Yes?"

I rapidly explained my predicament; I had to pass her class or I wouldn't be accepted to veterinary school. She glanced at her paper, fingered her peace symbol and peered down at the pitiful figure groveling at her feet. The people in line behind me looked away in disgust.

"You got a 58." "Yes, ma'am, I know." *"You also flunked the finals."* "Yes m'am, I know," I pleaded, "but I did the best I could. I was here every Saturday, as regular as an insulin shot." She paused. I held my breath. *"I'll pass you on one condition."* I looked her in the eye and said, "Anything!" I could picture myself doing her laundry all summer or chewing buffalo hides to make her new sandals.

Time froze . . .

"If you promise never to take Calculus or Trigonometry again."

I kissed her stickery ankles. She said, *"Next."*

IN DEFENSE OF THE CHICKEN

Everyone says they love chicken,
　　Ambrosia sent from above.
　　　　But nobody loves a chicken,
　　　　　　A chicken ain't easy to love.

　　　　It's hard to housebreak a chicken.
　　　　They just don't make very good pets.
　　You might teach one bird imitations
But that's 'bout as good as it gets.

　　　　Mentally, they're plumb light-headed
　　　　　And never confused by the facts.
　　　　That's why there's no seein' eye chickens,
　　　　　　Guard chickens or trained chicken acts.

　　　　　And everything tastes like chicken,
　　　　　From rattlesnake meat to fried bats.
　　It has anonymous flavor;
I figger they're all Democrats.

Some say this ignoble creature
　　With his intellect unrefined
　　　　And lack of civilized manners
　　　　　Has little to offer mankind.

　　　　But let me suggest, the chicken
　　　　Had two contributions to make;
　　The first was the peckin' order,
The second, the chicken-fried steak!

PRIDE

I'm closin' in on sixty with a vengeance, Mister Jim,
And I wouldn't ask no favors if I weren't out on a limb

> But it seems like no one's hirin'. Cowboyin's all I know
> And I worked for you a couple times, the last, not long ago.

It's been ten years? Oh, really? Well... I run into Buster Cole
And he said you might be lookin' so I gathered up my roll

> And bummed a ride off Buster. That's him a'waitin' in the car.
> I could go back to Brawley, but that seems so dadgum far!

Yeah, I know I quit ya last time but the winter froze me out.
My knees were always achin'. Think I had a touch of gout

> But now I'm sound and solid as a horseshoe, Mister Jim.
> You've got the place fixed up real nice, all lookin' neat and trim.

You painted the ol' bunkhouse! Man, I really liked it there.
Do ya still have Peg and Molly? Now, they were quite a pair.

> They could drag that big ol' hay sled through the snow just like a plow!
> Oh, she did? I'm really sorry. Guess ya feed with tractors now.

Ain't that Rocket! Good'a young horse as I started anywheres.
Who's ridin' all yer green stuff? Oh, you sold off all yer mares?

> If ya wanted we could git a couple yearlin's, split the cost.
> I'd be more than glad to...oh, sure. I just thought...Well, yer the boss,

But you still work cows a'horseback 'cause there ain't no other way
And fer that you need a cowboy, even one that's turnin' gray,

> And I'm yer man! You know me! You don't need my resume,
> Can ya put me in the bunkhouse, Mister Jim, whataya say?

A baler? Not on purpose...Me, I've always chased a cow.
Well, I 'preciate the offer but I think I'll pass for now.

> Give my best to your good missus. Yer divorced? The hell you are?
> I guess things are tough all over. C'mon, Buster, start the car!

HOME THE HARD WAY

They'd been out visiting friends in Wyoming for a week. Jesse'd had a good time but he was itchy to get back to the ranch near Lemmon, South Dakota. They pulled out Friday morning before daylight. Jesse drove...in self defense. His darlin' wife, for all her virtues, possessed an unerring sense of misdirection. North, to her, was a lisping Viking. West was what Elmer Fudd did when he was tired. She had trouble with the concept of distances. She'd heard of Miles Hare, Miles Standish and Miles Davis but she couldn't relate them to highway signs. She thought the odometer was aptly named.

By midafternoon Jesse was wore out. After cautiously checking the map he decided there was no way to get lost the rest of the way home so, reluctantly, he asked his wife to drive. He walked back to the little travel trailer they were pulling, threw her an encouraging wave and climbed in.

As she picked up speed Jesse peeled down to his shorts and lay on the bed. He was dreamin' of downed wire and water gaps when something woke him. They were stopped? He slid over to the door stepped out on the shoulder and walked around the end of the trailer. He took a peek and realized they were only at a stop sign at a sleepy little crossroads.

'At least we're not lost', he thought gratefully. Then he heard the crunch of gravel! In a desperate lunge he almost caught the aluminum awning strut, but he stepped on a bottle cap and skittered sideways like a bad billards shot!

He shouted and ran after her, mincing down the highway in a sort of plucked chicken ballet. She drove merrily off.

He stood along side a road, sore footed, white, embarrassed and hatless in his threadbare, holey Fruit of the Looms with the frayed elastic and baggy seat. He looked like Cupid gone to seed.

Jesse tiptoed over to the little collection of dilapidated buildings and borrowed a pair of old coveralls from a suspicious tradesman. He finally convinced this local that he was not an escaped lunatic and begged a ride home.

He didn't figger he could catch his wife so he directed this good Samaritan to a short cut. Jesse beat his wife home, tipped the wary driver, and went out to water the lawn.

She came whippin' up the driveway, saw him setting the sprinkler on the dry spot, and drove plum through the garage...without activating the automatic garage door opener, then derailed near the propane tank in the backyard!

It was a story that wasn't near as funny the first time he explained it to the insurance adjuster.

THE COWBOY AND THE DOCTOR

It all started when the boss said,

"Bring us more cattle!"

I was ridin' Reven Bubba, who's a son of Rev the Jets
A' way back in the crowdin' pen doin' pirouettes
And fillin' up the alley, pushin' cattle to the front
Whilst perfecting training methods that I'd cabbaged from Ray Hunt!

Now whoever'd built this crowdin' pen had built a real beaut
But it's obvious he'd never put a critter through a chute
'Cause once a cow had seen it, it was Katie bar the door!
And they wouldn't pass the portals if they'd been that way before

And this bunch was seasoned vet'rans! Bubba took another wrap
But they poured through him like water goes around a water gap!
They were floodin' all around us in this cowboy cul-de-sac
When a big ol' red-neck mamma mounted Bubba from the back!

Disbelief? No...more like terror showed in Bubba's bulging eyes!
He'd never liked the bunny hop, preferred to fraternize
With species of his color or at least his social class
So he rared straight up and nearly dumped this cowboy on his acetabulum!

My rope, tied to the saddle horn, uncoiled like a snake
And dallied round my boot (that I'd kicked free for safety's sake)
When a passing horned intruder speared my catch loop from the air.
In retrospect, I believe my luck was all downhill from there.

I'll spare the gruesome details 'cause you've heard'em all before.
Every cowboy's been a victim in this kind of tug-a-war.
Bein' caught between a buckin' horse who's finally jumped the fence
And a pig-eyed cow who stood her ground in sullen self defense.

I was somewhere in the middle as they dragged me back and forth
With my right arm wavin' Dixie and my boots a' pointin' north!
I was gettin' full of splinters and my clothes began to smoke
Like a Mexican reata...when the nylon finally broke!

It sounded like a gunshot! It exploded with such force
It jerked me ten feet high and threw me back upon my horse
Who promptly stuck his front feet in the dirt outside the gates
And fired me head first back amongst the frightened ungulates!

Ten thousand stompin' cattle hooves, all huntin' higher ground
Smashed me flatter'n a roadkill cat! So they hauled me into town
Where the doctor probed my mem'ry to determine the extent
Of the damage to my cranium. Was I broke or merely bent?...

☞

27

I awoke to see his tiny flashlight peerin' in my eyes.
He'd apparently detected life and begun to improvise
A test to check my brain involving triggernometry.
In a soothing voice he asked, "What's 97 minus 3?"

I stared back at him puzzled with a blank look in my eye.
"I'm afraid," the Doc concluded, "He's begun to stupify!"
I said, *"Doc! Just hold yer horses! This really ain't quite fair,*
I kin read a brand blindfolded just by feelin' of the hair!

I kin spot a raw imposter, be he saddlehorse or man
And always find Polaris, track a lizard through the sand,
I kin count a pen of cattle that comes poundin' through the gate
And never miss a single steer! I kin tell ya what they ate!

Ask me how to treat a pink-eye or who's winnin' All Around.
There's lots of stuff I savvy that'll prove my brain's still sound.
But yer concludin' that I'm daft upstairs, just a lamebrain buckaroo,
I'da passed yer test if you'da ask me somethin' that I knew!"

TINKER AND LADY

A stranger hangin' around cow workin's, sale barns or gatherin's might get the impression that little love exists between the cowboy and his dog. Only that the dog suffers from verbal abuse or that the cowboy is entitled to sue for mental exasperation! Neither is prone to open displays of affection. The cowboy acts tough and the dog acts bored.

But I remember one time up at the Grouse Creek Ranch. It was in the fall and we were workin' cows. Tinker was the cook. It wasn't that he was a great cook but he'd always done it and traditions get established regardless of their intrinsic worth. He made a big pot of chili and beans the first night. It was enough to feed the seven of us plus any visiting calvary platoon that might be billeting in the area! After supper we all loaded in the pickup and drove fifteen miles to Pop's ranch.

Pop had a natural hot springs on his place. We bathed and soaked, loaded up and drove back to our ranch. On arrival Tinker realized we'd left his little dog, Lady, back at Pop's. Nobody really worried but Tinker backtracked anyway. The rest of us slept peacefully (the chili and beans was fresh).

Next morning we stumbled into breakfast. The familiar aroma of chili and beans filled the kitchen. Unusual breakfast fare, but nobody said anything. Tinker looked like a dyin' duck in a thunderstorm! He'd been out all night lookin' for Lady.

Tinker was preoccupied all morning. He reheated the chili and beans for lunch. By supper (chili and beans) Tinker had become irritable. He'd walk to the window or outside every few minutes lookin' down the road and whistlin'. That night we slept with the doors and windows open in the bunkhouse.

At breakfast an unpleasant deja vu lay heavy over the table. The chili and beans was the consistency of South Dakota gumbo and smelled like burning brakes. Tinker spoke to no one . . . all day. For supper we had chili and bean sludge. It was the closest I've come to eating lava. That night we slept outside.

Complaining to the cook is bad cowboy etiquette, but we all agreed something had to be done. Had a submarine trained its sonar on our stomachs he'd have thought he was picking up a pod of nauseous killer whales!

Breakfast the third day was fried adobe that tasted vaguely of chili and beans. We ate in silence accompanied by the growling sounds of indigestion and explosive borborygmi. Then we heard a scratching at the door. Tinker jumped up and looked! There was Lady, sore footed, dusty and glad to be home! Tinker picked her up like a baby and hugged her. She licked his face.

Still holding her, he took a big T-bone steak out of the frig and slapped it in the frying pan. After a couple turns he put it on the floor in front of her. She ate all she could and lay down, exhausted. Needless to say, we were happy for them both but we tried to act like it was no big deal so Tinker wouldn't be embarrassed. After he left, we dove the bone!

GOOD BYE, OLD MAN

Somewhere deep in the old man's eyes a mem'ry took a'hold.
It fought the ageless undertow that drains and mocks the old.
I wiped a dribble off his chin, *"Pop, tell me what you see?"*
"It's all the boys I rode with, I think they've come for me."

Unconsciously I checked the door, *"It's nothin' but the wind.*
You better try and git some rest, tomorrow we'll go in."
"Is that you, Bob? I can't quite see. Yer mounted mighty well.
You never rode a horse that good when we were raisin' hell."

"Lie down, old man. There's no one here." ***"No, wait, that looks like Clyde.***
He helped me put ol' Blue to sleep. Why, hell, he even cried.
Now don't forget to check the salt, them cows'll drift back down.
Well, I'll be damned, there's Augustine, he worked here on the Brown

"When I hired on to buckaroo. . . But that's been fifty years."
The old man squinched his rheumy eyes, I dabbed away the tears.
The boss had told me he was old, had seen a lot of springs.
I bet ya if you peeled his bark, you'd count near eighty rings.

We'd rode the last three summers here together on the rim.
Just he and I, for puncher's pay. I'd learned a lot from him.
But now I'm settin' by his bed, uncertain what to do.
I ain't no good at nursin' coots. I'm only twenty-two.

"I reckon that I'm ready now. My friends are set to go.
They've got an extra mount cut out that's just for me, I know."
"You've got to stop this foolish talk! You shouldn't overdo!
Pop, all you need's a good night's sleep. You'll be as good as new."

"Don't make it complicated, kid, cut a pal some slack.
The saddle on that extra horse . . . that's my ol' weathered kak.
I'm comin', Bob, I'll be right there." He winked a misty eye
And tried to reach up for his hat, then died without a sigh.

I'll tellya, man, it freaked me out! I dang near come in two!
I'd never watched a person die, especially one I knew.
I tried to say a little prayer but all I knew was grace.
So I just said, *"Good Bye, Old Man,"* and covered up his face.

I poured myself the bitter dregs and stood out on the step.
Alone I listened to the night, as still as death, except,
I thought I heard above the coffee sloshin' in my cup
The far off, easy, pleasured sound of old friends catchin' up.

FEAR OF FLYING

Andy summed up flying the best I've heard, "If yer gonna have to land in a field, always land *with* the rows!"

Although I had a momentary lapse of good judgement once and took a week's worth of flying lessons, I have since left that task up to more serious folks. People who don't stay up all night celebrating and can actually reset the hands on a digital watch!

I know cowboys that are pilots. It's a frightening combination, akin to a CPA who does nude modeling on the side! All they talk about is flying and if there's two at your table, your brain goes numb after five minutes! It's like being trapped in a pickup on the road from Broadus to Billings between two cuttin' horse people!

But for good reason many western ranchers have taken up flying. They can check windmills, count cows and chase coyotes without having to open a gate. Roy hired a local boy out of Chadron to pilot him over his ranch to thin out the coyote population. The plane was a single engine Super Cub. The side door is dropped and the hunter straps himself in and leans out the door, cannon in hand. It is not a job for the faint hearted.

The pilot followed Roy's directions and was soon swooping down on the crafty coyotes while Roy blazed away with his twelve gauge. Suddenly the plane began to shake like a wet dog! The vibration loosened Roy's upper plate and the pilot's *I'd Rather Be Flying* tee shirt began to unravel! Roy, in his near-sighted exuberance, had led the coyote too much and shot the tip off of one propeller blade!

With heroic control, the young pilot landed the plane on an old stretch of rutted wagon road. He shut 'er down and staggered out into the sagebrush, visibly shaken.

He didn't care that he was twenty miles from the ranch headquarters and facin' a long walk back in the company of a crusty old rancher who had spit all over the side of his plane. He was just thankful to be on the ground!

His prayers were interrupted by an explosion! He dived for the dirt and smashed his new aviator sunglasses in the process! He looked back and Roy was standing in front of the plane holding the smoking twelve gauge.

"I evened 'em up, Sonny. She ought to fly okay now." He'd shot the tip off the other end of the prop!

Did they make it home? You bet yer shirt-tail they did! It vibrated a little bit, but no worse than drivin' down a railroad track at 120 mph!

ARE YOU A COWBOY?

When they ask, *"Are you a cowboy?"*
I kinda consider the source. . .
Is it someone who thinks I'm flush
And's tryin' to sell me a horse?

Or a downtown type in tennis shoes
Who's skeptical but courteous
And never smelled one of our kind
Up close, and's only curious.

The first guy really wants to know
Are you any good around stock?
Can you help a calvy heifer,
Can you dally and double hock?

You know how to use a bosal?
Can you mouth 'em and read a brand?
He never says it straight out loud
But he's askin', "Are you a hand?"

The other guy, who's just as nice,
Don't know a tit from a wattle!
And when he asks, "Are you for real?"
I quote the Greek, Aristotle,

Who might have answered had he lived
"Son, don't count on bein' lucky. . .
To find out if he lives with cows
Examine his boots for pucky!"

I like to think I'm good with cows,
A pretty fair hand with a horse
But am I a sure fire cowboy?
I'm dodgin' the answer, of course.

I've learned to handle the question
Whichever one wants to know it.
I ante up an say that I'm
A better cowboy poet!

Running M Half circle Flying 7 Quarter circle O Hatchet Bar Y Spur Lazy M Bench

A COWBOY'S HAT

The rules of the range are simple at best
  Should you venture in that habitat.
Don't cuss a man's dog, be good to the cook
  And don't mess with a cowboy's hat.

  Now I'll admit there's dogs that need cussin'
    And when Cookie starts out in the spring
  His grub ain't fit for buzzard consumption
    But a hat? That's a personal thing!

Sometimes it's all that a cowboy owns
  Or, at least, that he owns free and clear
So when someone suggests that he check it
  He'll prob'ly act like he didn't hear

  'Cause he'd no more think of leavin' his hat
    Than he'd consider crossin' a pard.
  Id be like a zebra leavin' his stripes
    Or a lawyer forgettin' his card!

In a dance hall, a court room or cafe
  If asked, he'll stick it under his chair
Or decide to himself if hats ain't welcome
  Then just maybe *he* shouldn't be there.

  He subscribes to a loose code of conduct
    That's unwritten but here's how it's said,
  "There's only one place that a hat belongs
    And that's settin' on top of yer head!"

If you're givin' some thought to my comments
  You'd expect an exception whereat
A place exists that's propitiously sound
  For a cowboy to take off his hat.

  If you're thinkin' a wedding, forget it!
    That's a half hitch a cowboy can't tie
  And if your final guess is a funeral,
    I can tellya friend, they never die!

So a word to the wise is sufficient
  And I guess I should leave it at that.
Suffice it to say, you can bum his last chew
  But don't mess with a cowboy's hat!
Repeat after me

  Don't mess with a cowboy's hat!

THE CAR WASH

I'm on my ninth pickup. Most of 'em have been Fords. No reason in particular. I wasn't rodeo hand enough to have a Dodge, farmer enough to drive an IH, or rich enough to own a Jimmy. I usually buy second hand vehicles. It's important that they be mechanically simple. I always thought it was a good sign when I could open the hood and see the road beneath the engine.

I've got a Ford and a Chevy now. Both of 'em 69's. It's a lot easier to work on the Ford, which is a great advantage. The Chevy's a little more crowded under the hood, but I never have to work on it anyhow, it just keeps runnin'. So I don't know which is the better truck.

My pickup's no different than the average farm truck. The driver's side cushion is wore through, one window roller is a Vise Grip. There are four gloves on the seat, none of 'em match. The jockey box is full of blinker lights, Phillips screws, electrical connections, needles, old syringes, valuable papers and extra keys to who knows what! Under the seat is a chain, a tree saw, a bird's nest, an official issue tire iron (unused), ant poison, a lumber store red flag and a University of Wyoming archaeological dig.

I never wash it. Lane learned that lesson the hard way. He pulled into the automatic car wash. Loretta took the dog and waited while Lane rode it through.

He sat there enjoyin' a moment's peace and marveled at the modern technology. He watched the soaper, then the big whirling brushes spin up the hood, climb the windshield and crawl over the cab. He remarked to himself how powerfully efficient, safe and virtually foolproof the machinery was. 'Amazin,' he smiled to himself. That was about the time the whirling dervish dropped into the bed of his pickup!

It sounded like a chain saw rippin' through a fifty-five gallon drum! Buckets, paint cans and an airplane wheel sailed out into the street like depth charges! Horseshoes, old bolts, pieces of a disassembled lawn mower carburetor, nails and a socket set shot through the air like machine gun fire!

The big brush squealed in pain as a steel fence post went through the observation window! The unit shorted out before the attendant called 911!

Lane spent four hours peelin' 300 yards of baler twine, 12 feet of hog wire, a log chain, two halters and a 35 foot nylon rope out of the equipment. By the time he got to sweepin' up, most of the Co-op dog food had dissolved and he could hose it out with the leaves and a half a bale of alfalfa.

Now, when he goes to the car wash he leaves his dog in the back of the pickup. Sort of an early warning device.

THE ELK HUNT

Lo, the weary hunter came
   No blood upon his hands.
His darlin' wife, in sweet relief
   Bid welcome to her man.

For ten long days he'd hunted
   From ridge to rocky stream
With sportsmen cronies like himself
   Alas, no elk was seen.

He told her how at daybreak
   They'd light out from the camp
And walk until their back and legs
   Were knotted in a cramp.

Then how around the campfire
   With reverence they would speak
About their wives and families
   Their plans for Holy Week,

Of politics and health food
   Of hunting as a sport,
Then just for therapeutic sake
   They'd have a little snort!

She bore his epic saga
   As wives are forced to bear
But winced when he said she forgot
   To pack his underwear.

She stilled the mighty hunter
   Her answer left him stunned,
"You must have overlooked them, dear,
   I packed'em with your gun!"

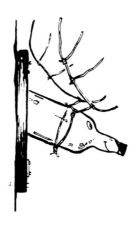

COW CHIP FILET

There's something that strikes me ironic
That borders on being abuse.
That's cooking steaks on a cow chip fire...
Like stewing you in your own juice!

I'm not sure where we got the idea!
I can think of no other case
Where a creature is finally rewarded
With such a back-handed slap in the face.

Even cavemen were more sympathetic.
There's no record they cooked on a stool
And as much as a mastodon munches
It couldn't have been lack of fuel!

I'm a great fan of barbecued chicken.
I savor the flavor and taste
But I don't think I'd be quite so eager
Were it cooked over dried poultry waste!

And as much as I like country spare ribs
I think that I might hesitate
Were they grilled over porcine torpedoes
From under the farrowing crate!

There are chips of all kinds in abundance
From poker to micro to munk
Yet the cow stands alone as a victim
To be fricasseed over a punk.

We can blame it all on the Indians,
Custom or westward migration
But putting yourself in a cow's place,
That's really not much consolation.

To put this whole thing in perspective
A comparable likeness would be
Cremating my cowboy carcass
On a pile of these poems wrote by me!

FATHER AND SON

I can't believe he's so ungrateful. I raised him from a pup!
　He worked beside me night and day. We never did let up.
He learned to drive a tractor, grease a windmill, pick up rock,
　To stack loose hay and irrigate and never watch the clock.

Then after school I'd teach him how to weld and sort the bolts
　And to add to his experience, I'd let him ride the colts,
Each summer he spent on the place beneath my watchful eye
　Then I sent him off to college thinkin' they would sanctify

All the learnin' I had give him but when he got out, guess what...
　He musta slept through classes 'cause he just flat come untaught
He's got all these new ideas about how to run the place.
　I've listened to his theories 'til I'm near a basket case!

He's subscribed to every magazine and leaves'em by my bed
　With pages marked for me to read 'bout how the cows are bred,
Or how to increase profits and to hedge the price we payed.
　Hell, he beats me up each mornin' and has the coffee made!

He quotes his old professors who, I'm sure ain't touched a plow.
　He forgets that twenty years ago I picked the kind of cow
We should be raisin', but he's so dang enthusiastic!
　And my imagination's lost what's left of it's elastic.

I like to think eventually we'll work this whole thing out
　And run this place together. Shoot, that's what farmin's all about.
And we might, if I survive these lengthy conversations
　And he don't lose his energy before I lose my patience!

DISAPPEARING DIGITS

When Winston Churchill and Richard Nixon made the victory sign, you probably thought the same thing I did . . . Them boys ain't team ropers!

Come to think of it, I've never seen a roper point at the TV camera and say "We're Number One"!

Ropers are at a definite disadvantage hitchhiking, buttoning a shirt and eating with chopsticks.

Many a roper has fished a finger out of his glove as a result of a slipshod dally. It always gives me a queasy feeling to see some roper on his hands and knees searching through the arena dirt like he was lookin' for a contact lens.

In any group of ropers you're liable to find a sampling of fellers who can't count to ten. Most take it in good stride and don't dwell on the handicap of missing a digit or two. It's the price you pay. As they say, "If you ain't been bucked off, cowboy, then you ain't been on many!"

I've still got all my fingers and thumbs but bein' a sorry roper has its advantages. You gotta catch 'em to lose 'em!

Losing a finger or thumb in the dally is no laughing matter. It's a lot more permanent than getting a haircut! Modern medicine and skilled surgeons can often replace the severed phalange. Of course, success of the operation depends on the condition of the missing piece and whether or not you can find it!

Young John walked into the emergency room with his hand wrapped in a towel.

"*What happened?*" the doctor asked.

"We were brandin' at the Pocket. I roped a calf and hung my thumb in the dally."

"*Well, let me see the piece you cut off,*" said the doc.

"I didn't bring it."

"*Do you know where it is? If it's in good shape we might be able to save it.*"

"Yeah, I do. But when it popped off, it sailed out over my horse's head pretty as you please. My good dog jumped up and snagged it in mid air!"

"*Great scott, son! Whyn't you shoot the dog?*"

"Shoot the dog!? He's the best one we got!"

BUFFALO TRACKS

As the typical cowman I've always been ambivalent about buffalo. I'd hate to see them become extinct but I've never had a burning desire to have a bunch in the field between my house and the road.

I've handled them a little and I've observed they can be stubborn. Sort of like trying to work a landslide! But buffalo raisers can become fanatics about their chosen species! They proffer several claims like low cholesterol, low fat meat and they are high on tradition.

I stayed one summer with Dan and Mary in Arizona. He built his house over a period of years and it looks like the Taj Mahal redecorated by Buffalo Bill! One of the features of which he is most proud is his collection of trophy heads hanging from the walls. I noticed that he had no buffalo skull. He had been such a gracious host, I vowed to remedy that deficiency. When I got home I called Roy in South Dakota who raises buffalo. I asked him to send my friend in Arizona a buffalo skull. I received the bill two weeks later and sat back to wait for an effusive thank you card. It never came.

The following summer I went to see Dan and Mary. The buffalo skull was nowhere in sight. We sat around drinking coffee and I waited for them to mention my gift. Finally I joked that what this house really needed was a buffalo skull. Mary turned to me like a bitin' dog! *"It was you!"* she accused!

Turns out that on that previous August, the post office had called and notified Mary of a pick up. They sounded urgent! It was 12 miles to the P.O., so she stopped by next morning on her way to work. The nervous mailmen hastily loaded a 3' by 3' heavy wooden crate in the back of her hatchback. Stenciled across the crate were the letters **S K U L**! Mary noted a peculiar odor. It was not entirely pleasant.

She drove 32 miles into Phoenix, parked and locked her car and went into work. The temperature that afternoon by the bank clock was 109°! By 5:30 p.m. a crowd had gathered in the parking lot to watch flies write "HELP ME" on the inside of her steamy windshield!

Mary drove home with the windows down and the hatchback up, covering her nose with her Peter Pan collar and gagging into her Pierre Cardin shirtsleeve!

Screeching to a halt in front of the Taj Mahal, this fashionably attired, stench-crazed woman clawed and tumbled the 60 lb. crate out of her car! It tore her left stocking and dripped black fluid on her ivory colored Dior imitation silk dress and open toed Gucci pumps! She grabbed a greasy tire iron from Dan's pickup and pried a board off the top! Peering up at her, with a blank look, was an eye!

I've never asked ol' Roy why he didn't skin the head. 'Course, I've never admitted to Mary that it was me who had sent it either. Sometimes it's best to let sleeping dogs lie!

GERALD TWO BEARS AND BILLY STRIKE

Gerald Two Bears was the foreman of the tribal branding crew.
Lots of Indians who were cowboys came to do what they could do.

Billy Strike was good at roping and his medicine was strong
And he roped'em automatic 'til misfortune came along!

He roped a good-size heifer calf, but he roped her 'round the neck.
She ran behind his horse's butt and put'em both in check!

The rope slid underneath his tail which spooked the pony some,
So, of course, he went to pitching! 'Cause the nylon chafed his bum!

Now like I said, that Billy's tough and wouldn't quit his dally,
The rope was holding him down tight! Made every peak and valley!

His horse was snorting up the dirt like he was sweepin' mines
And kickin' himself sideways like a spring when it unwinds!

Billy blew his left hand stirrup, so he leaned against the tide
But his saddle got some cockeyed, slippin' off the other side.

His dally peeled off the horn! His anchor chain had broke!
Billy flew like Humpty Dumpty and came down and broke his yolk!

Gerald Two Bears ran to Billy who lay still upon the ground.
He said, *"Billy, are you alright?"* Billy never made a sound.

He listened for his breathing but he lay so awfully still
He said, *"Billy, can you hear me?"* Then with superhuman will

Billy's eyelid raised, his eyeball turned and swiveled toward the source,
Gerald leaned up close and whispered, *"Billy, can I have your horse?"*

JANUARY, FEBRUARY, MUD

March comes in like a lion and goes out like a flat bed full of day-old Holstein calves. The most I can say about March is, it is a month of change. If March was a person, it would be an old man; cracked and weathered and cantankerous. Occasionally bearable but bent on maintaining his reputation for orneriness. The kind that won't turn up his hearing aid or zip his fly.

In the deep south March is pleasant. Matter of fact, they even look forward to it. But for most of cow country, the deep south might as well be on the back side of the moon! The March rain up here is not a gentle, life giving shower from Heaven to be savored and sniffed. It's more like the angels hosing out their hog confinement shed!

And the gentle breezes that whisper through the Houston pine trees aren't even a distant relative to the steady bone chilling 20 mph wind that whistles across eastern Idaho.

Even the word March is harsh and conjures up a tough, unforgiving image. Not like light and airy April or comfortable, short February. If I was asked to rename March, I would call it Mud. January, February, Mud...Mud 7, 1992...The Ides of Mud. Doesn't sound much different does it?

Mud is a busy time of the year; feedlots are full, calvin' has started and the lambin' crew is getting the jugs ready. Cowboys are still wearin' their winter long johns and five buckle overshoes. It's too soon to take the mud and snows off the pickup. The days are gettin' longer but nobody knows why.

The horses still have their hairy side out. It is usually the last month you can stick a tractor up to the axle.

What most people do in March is look forward to April.

"Well, one good thing about this miserable wind is it'll help dry up the mud."

"We'll be able to get into the fields next month."

"The bulk of the calvin' will be over in three or four weeks."

It seems I ought to have somethin' good to say about March. It's good and cold, good and windy, and good and long. Is that good enough?

I only knew one cowman who liked March; McQuilken. He said when it was over at least he still wouldn't have the whole winter to go through. He was just glad it didn't come in November.

FEAST OR FAMINE

In feast or famine, at least examine
the game we came to play
'Cause win or lose, it's how we use
the cards that come our way...

"Just let'er rain," the rancher said, "We've built up quite a thirst.
I know the low road's plum washed out, the tank dam's bound to burst.
We'll have to plant the wheat again and clean the water gaps
But you won't hear this fool complain if it reaches to my chaps!

The truth is, friends, we've needed this. We've been so dry so long
I thought I'd have to sell the cows and pay the piper's song.
The winter grass just lay there, stiff, for months it never changed.
I'd walk out through the cracklin' brown that covered all my range

And watch the wind blow dust clouds where the good grass shoulda been.
I'd count the bales in the stack and calculate again
The days of feedin' I had left before I'd have to face
The ultimate decision, what I'd do to save the place.

The weatherman was helpful, 'cept he always told the truth!
Piddlin' chance of ten percent meant it just rained in Duluth!
That's nice for Minnesota but it don't help me a bit,
I gave up chewin' Red Man so I wouldn't have to spit!

But he said last night, 'a chance of rain'. More than just a trace.
I washed the car and left the windows open just in case
And sure enough this mornin' big ol' clouds came rollin' in.
They parked above the driveway and the thunder made a din

That rattled all the winders in the house where I sat still.
And at two it started rainin'. I still ain't got my fill.
It's comin' down in buckets like its payin' back a debt,
Me? I'm standin' in the front yard, in my shorts and soakin' wet!

When the sun comes out tomorrow and sparkles all around
Off pools and puddles standin' like big diamonds on the ground
I'll remember feast or famine, but when it comes to rain
Ya take the feast when offered, if ya live out on the plain."

THE FLU

He had a little fever but he said he'd be okay.
"Too much to do to lay around and stay inside all day."
"Harry, you were up all night. You've been through a case of Halls!"
"I can't stay in the house all day! Gosh, what if someone calls!"

"You wouldn't have to answer it. I'd tell 'em you're outside."
"But what if Esther just dropped by. I'd have no place to hide."
"Don't fret yourself 'bout Esther, 'cause I'm meetin' her in town."
"I planned to fence the stackyard 'fore I move the cows on down."

"It's drizzlin' rain and freezin', you best lay there in your chair.
If someone comes just claim that you were workin' on the Fair."
"But they'll see I'm in my slippers! And what if I doze off?"
"All I know's you're sick and sufferin'. Just listen to that cough."

"Well, you go on with Esther and I'll try and close my eyes."
When she hit the yard that evening, she saw his compromise,
He was sittin' in the pickup, asleep there in the seat.
It was idlin' in the driveway. The dog made it complete,

Like he's just drove up, or maybe was fixin' to pull out.
Either way he had it covered in case someone might doubt
His constant perseverance, but his sweetheart only said,
"You can come on in now, darlin', it's safe to go to bed."

THE HIRED MAN

When they put him on the payroll
All the cowboys wondered "Why?"
'Cause he didn't own a saddle,
 Couldn't rope and didn't try!

        So they gave him all the bad jobs,
        The ones that they'd put off
        And went about their business
        Leavin' him to clean the trough

And irrigate. To fix the fence
And chop the thistle down
And when they all ran out of beer
Was him that went to town.

        He handled all the details
        The cowboys would ignore
        That held the place together,
        Kept the wolves back from the door.

They only saw him now and then,
At night when they'd come in
'Cause things were runnin' awful smooth
And they were busy men.

        Nobody ever noticed
        That he always did his part
        Until the day the windmill froze
        And the pickup wouldn't start!

The coyotes got the chickens
And the butane tank went dry.
The milk cow tore the barn down,
The mechanic's wife got high!

        Nobody'd stoked the wood stove
        Or started up a fire
        So the cook refused'em breakfast
        And threatened to retire!

The dogs tore up the smoke house
Like they'd hit it with a bomb!
The ranch ground to a stand still!
And the cowboys said, "Where's Tom?"

        Seems, they never really thought about
        How much they'd miss his face . . .
        It finally hit'em on the day
        The hired man quit the place!

THE GREAT CHICKEN RUN

Because of my peculiar qualifications I am asked to assist in some unconventional projects. Recently I served as a consultant on a semi-pro all-natural heavyweight chicken run.

Sam raises chickens. Not in a big way, but chickens are like records or cassettes; if yer gonna have one, you might as well have a bunch. Yet, old chickens present a problem. They cannot be retired gracefully. You might turn an old faithful horse out to pasture or stuff yer best bird dog. But a chicken, even in her twilight years, engenders very little loyalty or respect. Sam had a surplus of blue-haired layers that had lost their bloom.

A quick call to the local sale barn revealed that they had discontinued their Thursday afternoon chronic feeder chicken sale. Mr. Campbell (of noodle soup fame) and Mr. McNugget bought old hens, but only by the train carload. By a fortuitous conversation with a neighbor, Sam discovered that first generation immigrants from Viet Nam and other Southeast Asian countries prized the meat of mature chickens.

Armed with this information, Sam applied for a peddler's license. It was necessary for him to post a thousand dollar bond, in cash, to insure that the city collected its sales tax, which is not charged on live chickens anyway! No matter, Sam said it sorta took the free outta free enterprise.

Saturday morning we gathered all the old chickens in the neighborhood, plus a few grasshopper ducks and loaded them in the back of his Toyota pickup. Down the road we went with our convoy of foundering feathered fossils trailing duck down and chicken fluff like a cattail in the hands of a three-year-old! We pulled into the parking lot of MAI VAN'S ORIENTAL GROCERY AND UNUSUAL SEAFOOD.

We announced that we had live chickens for sale. Word spread like cheap wine on a white tuxedo! We were surrounded! Sam was dickerin' chickens, duckerin' ducks, peddlin' pullets and purveyin' poultry! I was the broiler bagman. Tyin' their scaley paws together as fast as Sam could catch 'em. One nice gentleman asked if we had any merganser ducks. I told 'im all we had was what we could catch at city park. He laughed, then asked about my dog. I changed the subject.

An attractive mother of three asked, through her six-year-old son, "How much for these five chickens?" Sam was naturally sympathetic for the young woman, trying to raise her family in a foreign land. He proffered $7 for all five. She countered with $6 and a tear. Sam settled for $5. Could we help her load them? She asked. Certainly! we said. We put a cardboard box with five live chickens in the trunk of her Lincoln Continental.

We sold 38 chickens, 2 roosters and 6 ducks, grossed $83, learned how to say "live chicken" in Vietnamese, Mong, Cambodian and Laotian, had a great time and fostered good will between two very different cultures. Not bad for a day's wok.

WOMEN!

She cried over the cat. After all that had happened she cried over the dang cat.

Christmas had been hectic. Feeding and watching out for 12 relatives for 5 days. Then in January when the blizzard hit I was at the state capital for a committee meeting. The power was out at the ranch and the water was off for 48 hours. She and the hired man managed to feed the cows but we lost four of them anyway. When I finally got through to her on the phone she said they were managing but hurry home if I could.

We held our little bull sale. She did the programs, mailed the flyers, planned the lunch and smiled at prospective buyers for a day and a half. It went smoothly but she didn't get much rest that week.

It rained in March. The new calves got the scours. I was calvin' so she sorta took over treating the calves. She divided her time between haulin' the kids back and forth to town and nursin' sick calves.

Right before the regional track meet our oldest broke his leg. He was bitterly disappointed and was bedridden for two weeks. She waited on him hand and foot.

At our brandin' she fed 34 people outta the back of the pickup in the far pasture.

The first day it got over 85° she went to town for parts. On the way home her car broke down and she walked the last four miles. Her crock pot shorted out and the beans froze to the bottom. That was the night the school superintendent dropped by.

Well, she finally went to the doctor about the pain in her hands. Arthritis. Sorta what she'd suspected all along. Gettin' older.

In the last six months we've had two car wrecks, the well pump went out, my mother came to live with us, we found a leak in the roof above the kitchen sink, gophers got in her garden, the meat freezer gave up the ghost, I sold her favorite cow, our insurance went up, I started takin' high blood pressure pills and they cancelled her favorite TV show.

It's been kind of a tough go at our place these last few months. But she never complained. Just bowed her back and kept goin'.

We had company last night. After they left, this morning we found the cat dead in the driveway. A black tom cat. One of the barn cats. I didn't even know she cared about him. He hardly ever came in the house.

I found her in the bedroom cryin' her eyes out. "The cat?" I asked. She nodded. I held her.

Women cry over the strangest things.

CHAUVINIST?   WHO ME?

When I suggested she do dishes and later stoke the fire
    Because I felt that was her proper place
She calmly took the custard pie and the plate of pickled beets
    And used it to redecorate my face!

Now I know this sounds unsavory in this modern day and age
    When male sensitivity is in
But I think it's biological, congenital at best,
    'Cause women see things differently than men.

Like the importance of a curtain or fragrance in the air
    Or, yes, the omnipresent potted plants.
They concern themselves with beauty and a certain ambience
    While I'm content to spray the place for ants!

In fairness to my jackass friends, it's not true that we don't care.
    We're lookin' from a different point of view.
And to illustrate my reasoning and perhaps to shed some light
    I offer this example as a clue,

I was sitting with a couple when I heard the man remark
    "My dear, I think I've seen that dress before."
"Yes, you have. I was wearing it the last time we went out.
    I believe...it was 1984."

Then she chastised him severely and I'm sure she had a point,
    And I'll admit her wisdom right up front.
But my simple cowboy logic led me down a different path
    Like blindmen feelin' up the elephant!

If women understood our thinkin' they might cut us all some slack
    And maybe their attitude might soften.
When he recognized his spouse's dress, the thought occurred to me...
    The crazy fool's takin' her out too often!

THE COWBOY'S GUIDE TO VEGETARIANS

In an effort to foster an understanding between cowboys and vegetarians, it is crucial to debunk certain myths.

Myth No. 1 - *Vegetarians are all left wing, liberal Democrats who were hippies in the '60s.*

Not so. The average age of a 1992 vegetarian is 35. So in 1964 they would have been eight years old. They were being forced to clean their plate ("but Mom, I don't like broccoli!") before they could have dessert.

It was not until President Bush came out of the closet and announced his dislike for broccoli that he found a cause some vegetarians could rally behind! Three registered as Republicans!

Myth No. 2 - *Vegetarians have no sense of humor.*

This myth is still under study. It appears that vegetarians see very little humor in cows being accused of belching huge quantities of methane into the atmosphere. But they get a chuckle when someone throws ketchup on a mink coat. It just goes to show that what is funny depends on whose ox (or kumquat) is being gored.

Myth No. 3 - *Vegetarians are a vanishing breed.*

An interesting myth. They are holding their own, approximately three percent of the U.S. population. But the turnover is high. The percentage is also affected by immigrants, ethnic minorities and the poor. As they improve their lifestyle they feed their family more meat.

In a constant effort to maintain their ranks, vegetarians align themselves with like-minded groups who help them vegetate; New Age trade shows, Psychic conventions and the Hare Krishna.

Myth No. 4 - *Most vegetarians became vegetarians because their mother said liver was good for them.*

As good a reason as any, but not necessarily so. Snoopy, Garfield and Mickey had more influence than mom. These were animals who ate chocolate chip cookies and lasagna. They could sing and they knew Annette Funicello. They could speak and go to heaven. It followed that Porky Pig and Foghorn Leghorn had human feelings too and didn't relish being eaten. Vegetarians feel sorry for drumsticks and Baco Bits.

Myth No. 5 - *All vegetarians are alike.*

Wrong again! Some vegetarians eat fish and chicken

Others will eat only eggs and milk. That's a practical decision, I suspect. One can pass up a Spam sandwich or a bowl of menudo but it's not so easy to turn down chocolate mint ice cream.

And there is a small group of true believers who eschew even the wearing of wool or leather. They are easily identified wearing petrochemical derivatives and a plastic shower cap!

A VEGETARIAN'S GUIDE TO COWBOYS

Many myths have been promulgated that have fostered a misunderstanding of cowboys by herbivores. It is incumbent on me to shed some light on this subject for my vegetarian friends.

Myth No. 1 - *Cowboys are mean to cows.*

This myth may be reinforced by the cowboy's habit of roping cows for sport, branding their young and primping them like poodles at livestock shows. But in their defense, these practices are done without malice. Just sort of the usual predator/prey relationship, like parents with children enrolled in organized sports.

Myth No. 2 - *Cowboys are right wing political fanatics.*

Cowboys are suspicious of politicians and, like most Americans, don't vote either. They hold to a muddled Code of the West that forbids associating with known feminists but allows kissing your horse. Very confusing.

Myth No. 3 - *Cows hate cowboys.*

Cows have an IQ somewhere between a cedar post and a sandhill crane. It is unlikely that they lay awake nights plotting revenge. However, fate has made the cow and cowboy dependent on each other. The same unnatural relationship that exists between politicians and newspaper reporters or lawyers and criminals.

Myth No. 4 - *Cowboys are a vanishing breed.*

As long as 97 percent of the population eats meat, there will be cows and as long as there are cows, there will be cowboys. However, they **are** hard to see from the freeway.

Myth No. 5 - *Cowboys eat beef everyday.*

Or buffalo wings, pigs feet or cheek meat off an old ewe! They'll even eat hay if you put enough whiskey on it. Actually they'll eat most anything the cook serves up though I've never seen 'em eat a snail darter or a spotted owl!

Myth No. 6 - *Cowboys are not like the romantic image portrayed in Marlboro commercials and John Wayne movies.*

Of course they are! 'Specially if you catch 'em between gettin' bucked off before breakfast and losin' their lunch on the way home from the dance.

THE OYSTER

The sign upon the cafe wall said OYSTERS: fifty cents.
"How quaint," the blue-eyed sweetheart said with some bewildermence,
"I didn't know they served such fare out here upon the plain."
"Oh, sure," her cowboy date replied, "We're really quite urbane."

"I would guess they're Chesapeake or Blue Point, don 't you think?"
"No ma'am, they're mostly Hereford cross . . . and usually they're pink
But I've been cold, so cold myself, what you say could be true
And if a man looked close enough, their points could sure be blue!"

She said, *"I gather them myself out on the bay alone.*
I pluck them from the murky depths and smash them with a stone!"
The cowboy winced, imagining a calf with her beneath,
"Me, I use a pocket knife and yank'em with my teeth."

"Oh, my," she said, *"You animal! How crude and unrefined!*
Your masculine assertiveness sends shivers up my spine!
But I prefer a butcher knife too dull to really cut.
I wedge it in on either side and crack it like a nut!

I pry them out. If they resist, sometimes I use the pliers
Or even Grandpa's pruning shears if that's what it requires!"
The hair stood on the cowboy's neck. His stomach did a whirl.
He'd never heard such grisly talk, especially from a girl!

"I like them fresh," the sweetheart said and laid her menu down
Then ordered oysters for them both when the waiter came around.
The cowboy smiled gamely, though her words stuck in his craw
But he finally fainted dead away when she said, *"I'll have mine raw!"*

62

THE AG TRIVIA QUIZ

Circle the most correct answer.

1. BLACK BALDY
a) an aging basketball player
b) a Brangus who combs his hair over the bald spot
c) the author of this book

2. U.S.D.A.
a) the arm of H.E.W. that dispenses food stamps
b) a warehouse to store wheat and cheese
c) the government's alternative to organized agriculture

3. CHRONIC STEER
a) a hypochondriac
b) a perpetual whiner
c) a feedlot animal that lives forever

4. PROFIT
a) a new word
b) one who predicts the future
c) as elusive as a generous banker

5. A LITTLE EAR
a) someone who can't carry a tune
b) what frogs have
c) defective corn

6. PERFORMANCE TESTED
a) how fast a bull can run the 100-yard dash
b) a good loan risk
c) a man with eight kids

7. ANIMAL RIGHTS
a) a dog that can go anywhere he wants
b) initiation ceremony for the L.A. Raiders
c) does not apply to small rodents and cowboys

8. EXTENSION AGENT
a) a preservative used in hot dogs
b) a ladder salesman
c) that telescoping device on the end of a Roto Rooter

9. D.V.M.
a) Department of Motor Vehicles
b) dip vat manager
c) a license to be late everywhere you go

10. HOG FINISHING EQUIPMENT
a) an electric sander
b) sausage grinder
c) lipstick in a sleazy bar

11. GOOD PASTURE
a) the Sandhills to a rancher
b) corn stubble to a farmer
c) shag carpet to a goat man

12. SALT LICK
a) where cows gather to gossip
b) a new Olympic event using postage stamps and a salt shaker
c) what Salt Lake City is gonna be if the lake keeps risin'

13. CHECK-OFF
a) a practice that discriminates against people from Prague
b) a chess move
c) roll call at Purina Mills

14. #2 OKIE
a) second string quarterback at Oklahoma State University
b) the Lieutenant Governor of Oklahoma
c) one who made it as far as Bakersfield

15. OPEN COW
a) one that is gullible to suggestion
b) the name of Wendy's new burger
c) instructions for doing a cesarean

16. FUTURES MARKET
a) a place to buy calendars
b) science fiction bookstore
c) another method of losing money

17. POLLED COW
a) a one that is turned out near the north pole
b) raised in Poland
c) one that has been contacted by George Gallup

18. N.C.A.
a) Northern California Accountants
b) No Comment Association
c) Never Convicted Auctioneers

19. RUMINANTS
a) true vegetarians
b) men who gather in coffee shops
c) a motel that furnishes ants in each room

20. DEHORN
a) grounding your teenage son
b) takin' the honk out of a bull
c) an appendage on de head

21. SCOURS
a) what you do with steel wool
b) the name of a new deodorant soap
c) a bad thing to have on a crowded bus

22. HORTICULTURE
a) a cult of agronomists
b) a women's self improvement group
c) an unfortunate title for a good profession

23. ORDER BUYER
a) a person who delivers groceries to shut-ins
b) a parolee with your blank check
c) how sale barns unload their dead and dying

24. FOOT ROT
a) ruler erosion
b) what happens when yer socks disintegrate and the elastic builds up around yer ankles
c) a disease of columnists that results from putting their feet in their mouths too often

25. IVERMEC
a) a resort in the Swiss Alps
b) Merck's retirement program
c) last winner of the Triple Crown

26. WATTLE
a) the gait of a foundered duck
b) stuff that builds up in your pocketknife
c) a cow handle

27. YELLOWHEAD
a) a disease of turkeys
b) a major Canadian highway
c) a species of catfish

28. DISPLACED ABOMASUM
a) a homeless bedouin
b) a missing lawnmower part
c) the result of chronic Mexican food consumption

29. RETAINED OWNERSHIP
a) a method of prolonging the unknown
b) what happens when your cat has kittens
c) like retained placenta

30. BOG SPAVIN
a) a swelling in the hock
b) middle linebacker for the Seattle Seahawks
c) a tool to train dogs with

31. TWO-INCH BALL
a) a bumper attachment
b) a short cry
c) a small dance floor

32. MARTINGALE
a) a California equine accoutrement
b) Hermaphrodite twin calf
c) preg checker's tendonitis

33. HANGIN' TENDER
a) an obscure cut of beef
b) an unreleased Elvis recording
c) how sloths make love

34. BALLISTOVET
a) injecting livestock with darts
b) a disease of vets caused by wearing wet socks
c) a drink you can order at the V.F.W.

35. FREE TRADE
a) a trick Canada and the United States think they played on each other
b) a purchase circumventing the auction barn
c) when two purebred breeders buy each other's $150,000 bull

36. PLUCK
a) a packinghouse term
b) a good attribute in barrel racers
c) the sound a cow pie makes when it hits the ground

37. ERGOT
a) a nasty fungus
b) French inventor of the emesis basin
c) the color of feedlot coffee with non-dairy creamer

38. HOLISTIC APPROACH
a) an environmental grazing method
b) a Jehovah's Witness comin' up your drive
c) your fourth putt

39. FISTULOUS WITHERS
a) sick feeder lambs
b) cowboy poet from 18th century England
c) a good reason to sell your horse

40. SALORN
a) a new breed of cattle
b) shumthin' yoo dally on
c) the callus on your pencil finger

41. BLUE HEELER
a) supreme cow dog
b) a team roper outta the money
c) Oral Roberts on a bad day

42. NARES
a) nose tong attachment
b) unused holes in your belt
c) Australian marsupials

43. CABRITO
a) the newest Chevrolet sports car
b) barbecued goat
c) the hairs on the end of your nose

44. GOMER
a) a bull with no follow-through
b) an ancient sport involving a piggin' string, two chickens and a chocolate shake
c) a secondary irrigation tributary

THE STOCKDOG DEMONSTRATION

Pete was invited to put on a working stockdog demonstration at the agricultural fair in the nearby town of Perdue, Saskatchewan. He could have brought his own lambs that were "dog wise" but his hosts offered to furnish the sheep.

On arrival in Perdue that morning Pete peeked into the dark trailer at the sheep. Six big black-headed Suffolk ewes glared back at him malevolently. It was like looking into a cave full of bank examiners! He stationed his wife Pam and his dog Jock at the back and opened the tailgate. The ewes charged in a flying wedge and bowled over the defense!

They made straight for the show barn then turned at the last second for a windbreak of willers. Jock was on 'em, snapping at their noses! In the melee an abscess broke on one of the ewes!

The ewes holed up in the windbreak . . . all save one who started down the highway to town. Pete sent Jock "away to me" to fetch 'er back. The two met three times on the center line before she turned back for the bunch. She arrived with a bloody snoot and led the others down the road in the opposite direction!

Assuming control, Pete, Pam and Jock aimed for the intersection leading back into the fairgrounds. It was fenced on both sides except for one driveway that led to a nice country home set back on a beautifully landscaped lawn. The ewes took a hard right and made for the house!

As the flock rounded the corner of the house, Pete caught a glimpse of a well-dressed lady peeking through the curtain. They made twelve passes around the house trampling shrubs, lawn and manicured flower beds. They mangled four bicycles and knocked over six flower pots before panting to a slippery stop on the front porch! The porch floor looked like the bottom of a dumpster!

The enraged homeowner opened the door to register her displeasure. The lead ewe broke for the living room! Pete followed, slamming the door behind him!

They raced over sofas, coffee tables, potted plants, under the kitchen table, through the hall and back to the living room where the ewe paused to squat on the shag carpet (beige, of course) in front of the television set!

Pete caught a hind leg and drug her across the rug toward the door. Just as he raised his hand to say, *"No, don't..."*, the helpful homeowner jerked open the door admitting Ewe Number Two!

In small towns like Perdue news travels fast. It was standing room only for the working stockdog demonstration that afternoon!

SHEEPMEN, BORDER COLLIES AND MULES

What do sheepmen, border collies and mules have in common with blue heelers, horses and cowboys? Nothing! Except that I've seen each one of 'em on all fours at one time or another, they seem to have nothing in common.

They are two distinct groups of species that are as different as mint jelly and Co-op dog food. Back in the Pleistocene Age, *Homo carnivorous* came to an evolutionary fork in the road. One group, staff in hand, took its livestock and beasts of burden and walked left. The other, rope in hand, headed west astride its beast of burden, accompanied by its livestock and pets.

Think back on the mules you have known personally. Did you ever know a stupid one? No. Did you ever know a stubborn, sly, mean or snobbish one? Probably. People don't really own mules, anymore than they 'own' cats. A mule operates at about the same belligerence level as a cowman, which explains why the two don't get along. A sheepman will tolerate a smart ass as long as he'll pull the camp or pack the pots and pans. The cowboy insists on showing the mule who's boss.

Horses, on the other hand, have more frivolous personalities which bother sheepmen. Fun, in any form, makes sheepmen nervous. Did I say nervous? That brings us to one of the most amazing genetic creations on earth, the border collie! With the energy of a hummingbird, the work ethic of a boat person and the loyalty of Lassie, they are a miraculous animal. The more complicated the signals, the more uncooperative the livestock, the more they like it. Instinct and endless hours of training required by dog and master make them ideally suited for each other. They are as serious as a root canal!

The cowboy has no patience for the details of dog training. He didn't take much schooling to be a cowboy, so he figgers the blue heeler shouldn't need much training to be a cowdog. It's sort of a "hike it to me and go out for a pass" type of working relationship. Giving a good border collie to a cowboy would be like giving a food processor to a caveman!

But what happens when a rancher decides to raise both sheep and cattle? A mutant is created. He becomes uncertain. The sheep side of his brain tells him to vote Republican, attend educational meetings, eat the heel and pay in cash. The cow side of his brain keeps whispering he should get in the race horse business and buy drinks for the house.

Maybe the sheepman and cowman will eventually blend into some bland bureaucratic animal husbandryman without any sharp edges. Like a fast food salad bar where you can't tell the Thousand Island from the Blue Cheese. Personally, I'd hate to see that. I like sharp edges.

68

ONEUPSMANSHIP

No tellin' how many good dogs he outlived,
No matter how good your dog was
He'd once had a collie, a heeler or gyp
That did everything your dog does

And more! The same for horses and pickup trucks
Though the one he drove was a wreck.
The best I could tell, he didn't have nothin'
But I've never seen that affect

His opinion on anything you mighta owned
From a purebred bull to a bit!
By the time he'd finished pontificatin',
You'd wind up suckin' hind tit!

Last night I was braggin' on one of my dogs
I'd sold at the top of the year
To a herder who worked on Basabe's ranch.
They said my dog had no peer.

It was seven miles of circuitous road
From the lower field to the lane.
They'd send my good collie to bring the sheep home
And never had call to complain.

He'd start'em out where the new highway sign warned,
CAUTION: LIVESTOCK CROSSING AHEAD,
Then herd'em north to the Conoco billboard,
Go right 'til a homemade sign read

POLOMBO'S TOMATOES AND VEGETABLE STAND
Where he'd turn toward the four-way stop.
Platteville read $\boxed{\text{EAST} \Rightarrow}$, so he'd go 'til he spotted
DICK'S WELDING AND SHEET METAL SHOP.

Take a left on Bromley then up past the barn
That advertised HAY BY THE BALE
'Til at last he turned up the Willow Creek Road
By the sign that said RABBITS FOR SALE.

At the third mailbox sayin' BASABE SHEEP
He'd fetch'em just like he'd been shown
And drive that big bunch of scatterbrained woolies
Up the lane, just him, all alone.

'Top that!' I thought, 'You cranky ol' coot!' He said
"That's mighty impressive indeed!
Though I'm not surprised 'cause my dog spent last year
Teachin' all them sheep how to read!"

THE SHEEPMAN

There's a lot to be said for the sheepman
   That ain't been written in books.
Like the kinda dog that he carries
   Or the squinty way that he looks.

He figgers all creatures are coyotes
   If they walk on two legs or four.
He don't call it a 'B.L.M. meeting'
   He thinks of it more like a war!

He's wary of folks who dress flashy
   And offer to pick up the tab.
He'd rather go dutch or go hungry
   Than owe some tin god of the gab.

Hist'ry ain't made him a hero
   John Wayne ain't made him a saint
But he's still out there on the allotment
   Survivin' when cowboys cain't.

He's a squatter in all of the movies
   The butt of the cowboy's jokes
A token on all of the Meat Boards
   The wheel ox in all of the yokes.

And he suffers it all with a silence
   So you'd think his powder is damp
But when he speaks, it's with a conviction
   That I learned first hand in his camp.

See, I've spent some time around sheepmen
   And I've learned this fact about him
If the bugger calls and then raises...
   Your chances of winnin' are slim.

THE SHEEPHERDER'S LAMENT

by Baxter and Pinto Bennett

I had her out here in my sheep camp
    Pullin' wool over her eyes.
I just about had her enchanted
    Had her believin' my lies

    But something went wrong when I told her
        We couldn't get married 'til June.
    She was welcome to stay through the winter,
        I loved her but she wised up too soon.

The next one I had wasn't pretty
    But she cooked and sewed her own clothes.
Lord knows, I've never been choosey
    But she could slice cheese with her nose!

    She was heavy but that didn't matter,
        Looked good in the dark of the moon.
    She hung around here 'til November,
        I loved her but she wised up too soon.

There was Nadine and Flossie and Alice,
    Stella and a couple named Ruth
But one thing they all had in common,
    Almost all were long in the tooth!

    I've been out here for twenty-five winters
        Not one of 'em made it 'til June
    I don't mean that they were all losers,
        I loved 'em but they wised up too soon.

I never ask much from my women,
    Feed the dog, put wine in my cup
And never ask too many questions,
    Drive home and never wise up!

THE MAPLE CREEK OPEN

The scene was the annual stockdog trials
    At Maple Creek, Saskatchewan.
All the sheepmen for miles had come for the trials
    And brought a dog he would matchewan.

Then a stranger pulled up to the fence,
    "New Meat," the locals were hopin'.
From the back of his truck he drug out ol' Tuck
    And entered him up in the Open.

The Open was after the Novice.
    The good dogs all put on a show.
They were reachin' and stretchin', liftin' and fetchin'
    And givin' each other a go!

Then last but not least came ol' Tuck
    And he did right well, 'til the end
And he woulda done better, if he'd quit when he shed'er,
    But he ate the last ewe that he penned!

I mean, right there in front of the judge!
    Just like a boa constrictor!
He looked happy indeed as he spit out a seed*
    And savored the spoils of the victor.

"Disqualified!" screamed the contestants.
    Their objections were loud and profane.
Tuck watched all the while with his lanolin smile
    While his master begged time to explain,

"I see that wee Tuck has offended
    With his indiscriminate zeal
I regret his bad taste but no one's disgraced,
    So he ate an ol' ewe. . . no big deal!

"Lord knows I've tried to teach him good manners
    But you've got to admit that ol' sheep
Was tough as a shoe an' dang hard to chew
    But Tuck never complained. . . not a peep!

"I'm sorry he partook yer pore darlin'
    He did only what he thought was right
From tail to head, he's Canadian bred,
    He ate her to just be polite!"

* sheep have little seeds, ya know. You see'em
scattered all over the ground wherever sheep are.

74

ON THE EDGE OF COMMON SENSE
Baxter Black DVM

by Boller

Hi frendz and felo cowdogz, I, Baxter's faythfull unaprizeated 'good dog' and bezt frend, have subsutooted my collum for his. Becase he takes grate delite in piken on mans best frend, us, the all Amerakin cowdog. I cannt tell yoo how much monny he haz made riding on hour name..."Go git In The Pikup, Yoo..." Ha, ha, funny as a pech pite in the Gravy Trane!

Lemme tell yoo, I hang out with thes trkey and he is not the cowboy he clame. The onely whay he can rop a hefer is buy chacing her so long, she falls from egzoshchon. He likes to make okayzhenal refrens to his veteranary skills. Hour ranch iz the onely plase I no that has les than ten cows and the rendering truk stops evreday!

The real seekret to the sekses of hour cattel opperashon is me, ofe corse! Do yoo think a cowboy cood fined a cow in the brush with out uz? Are yoo cedden! Thay ride a long like thay no where ther going but we no there just foloing us.

Thay acte like ther doen uz a faver buy letten us ride into towen. Ther just to laze to clen the junk outa the pikup bed. So we gota sit and garde it while pate each outher on the back at the coffe shop.

All for what? Stak bones and cavear? Rong, bisket lips! Yoo ever eat Coop dog food? It tasts like chiken and gives me gas.

Its time we stood on all fors and be cownted! We perform many vitel servesess on the ranch but Bumbling Black had the awdasety to tell a reporter I wus a prop! I wood like yoo to send me fotografik evadens of uz doing hour doote. Sort of "Cow Dogs in Akshon". Sports Elastrated mite even do a pese on uz.

Male yore foto to:

Boller
% Cowdog Hall of Champenz
box 190
Brighten, CO 80601

footnote: Baxter writes a weekly column. A while back his dog, Boller, intercepted the mail and substituted his own column. Boller received many letters from cowdogs sympathetic to his plight. Needless to say, he lost them all.

DIVERSIFIED FARMING

*'Wheat is down
to two dollars...
I should'a sold it
last fall.*

*Calves are over
a dollar...
I think I'll hold on
to'em all!'*

THE FIRST COUNTY AGENT

Clarence of Euphrates was just a simple man
He graduated ag school from Tigress A&M

It only took him seven days to garner his degree
But days were longer then, of course, and no one took P.E.

His goals were really modest; to help clean up the air
To save the world from ignorance, become a millionaire

To always strive for excellence and never be complacent
So Clarence of Euphrates became a county agent

His first job was a garden, the year was 2 A.S.
To clarify, that's After Snake, and Eden was a mess!

He organized the fair board though his paperwork was slow
And told the state director no more than he should know

His achievements in 4-H work were a credit to the kids
On a field trip to Egypt they built the pyramids

The local folks would cringe in fear and hide out in the thickets
'Cause everytime that Clarence came, he'd sell'em raffle tickets!

In the Eden County Stockmens he was honored by his peers
And served as secretary for seven hundred years

He put on endless meetings and countless demonstrations
With faulty slide projectors and drafty ventilations

He wrote a million pamphlets, read record books galore
And patted pigs and lambs and kids 'til his hands and heart were sore.

He always judged the apple pies at Eden County Fair
Although the ancient legends warned of apples, to beware

But Clarence ate'm anyway and scoffed at their reaction
But alas, he finally died, of apple pie compaction.

FARMER OR RANCHER?

There is a distinction in the livestock business between ranchers and farmers. But how does a city slicker tell the difference? I have some guidelines that should be helpful.

1. Ranchers live in the west. Except beet growers in Idaho, cotton farmers in Arizona, prune pickers in California and wheat producers in Montana. Farmers live east of Burlington, Colorado. Except for cattle ranchers in the Sandhills of Nebraska, cracker cowboys in Florida, Flinthills cowmen in Kansas, and mink ranchers in Michigan.

2. Farmers wear seed company caps except when they're attending the PCA banquet, the annual cattlemen's meeting or going on a tour to a foreign country. Ranchers wear western hats except when they're roping, putting up hay or feeding cows at 30° below zero.

3. Ranchers wear western boots except when they're irrigating and sleeping. Farmers wear western boots except when they go to town.

4. Farmers work cows afoot, on a tractor, a four-wheeler, a motorcycle, in the pickup, snowmobile, road-grader, canoe or ultralight. Virtually any motorized contraption except a horse. Ranchers work cows horseback.

5. Farmers can identify grass. Ranchers have trouble distinguishing grass from weeds and indoor-outdoor carpet. Farmers think grass is green. Ranchers think it is yellow.

6. Ranchers haul their dogs around in the pickup and pretend they are stock dogs. Farmers usually leave their pets at home.

7. Farmers think a rope is good for towing farm equipment, tying down bales and staking the milk cow along the highway. A rancher's rope hangs on the saddle and is only used to throw at critters.

8. A rancher wouldn't be caught dead in overalls. A farmer never wears a scarf or spurs.

9. Farmers complain about the weather, the market, the government, the banker, taxes, county roads, the price of seed, equipment, veterinary work, pickups, tires and kids. So do ranchers.

Now that I've made it perfectly clear, let's assume you see a man on Main Street in Enid, Oklahoma. He's wearing western boots, a seed corn cap and has a pocketful of pencils. He's driving his pickup complete with a dog, a saddle and a four-wheeler in the back. Which is he, a farmer or rancher?

He's either a rancher on his way to a roping or a farmer coming back from the flea market. The only way to be sure is to examine his rope. If it has more than two knots in it, he's a farmer!

EAT MORE BEEF!

I'm a fairly frequent victim of the EAT MORE BEEF! campaign.
    I've read the ads and seen the spots intended to explain
That if I will eat real beef, I will be real people
    And have more iron inside me than a rusty army Jeep'll!

It will make me thin and happy and put my life in order
    And I agree in principle, I've been a staunch supporter.
But sometimes all this hoopelah just plain gives me the jitters.
    See, I have a vested interest. I raise the blasted critters!

Which tends to make me cynical, to doubt or even scoff it!
    'Cause from a cowman's point of view, it ain't all fun and profit.
They've crippled more than one good horse and countless good blue heelers,
    An order buyer now and then, plus hordes of wheeler dealers!

And as for me, I've had my share of wounds and lacerations,
    Of broken heads and swollen thumbs, unwelcome perforations.
They've knocked me down and knocked me out and overhauled my keister
    And woke me up on Christmas day and kept me up 'til Easter!

They've embarrassed and ignored me, annoyed and misused me.
    They've broke me flat as hammered pie, mistreated and abused me,
And yet I keep on comin' back like bees keep makin' honey.
    Maybe I'm a masochist 'cause it dang sure ain't the money!

So when they tell me EAT MORE BEEF!, I'll try and be attentive.
    But tellin' me's a waste of time, I've got my own incentive.
I've spent a lifetime workin' cows which keeps a man believin'.
    You bet yer life I EAT MORE BEEF! . . . I eat it to get even!

THE EPITAPH

That ol' man could sure set a post. Three foot down
        in the hardest ground, grunt and thud, chink and chime.
Bedrock trembled beneath his bar. Each new whack
        broke the back of granite old as time.

Be easier to move it. The hole, that is.
        But that wasn't his way of settin' a post.
His ran like a soldier's backbone, straight as a die
        to the naked eye. Perfect . . . not just close.

He'd scoop the dirt into it in a careful way.
        Like sculptor's clay he'd add an inch or two.
"Each one counts," he'd say to me, then tamp that thing
        'til the bar would ring and the earth was black and blue.

He set cedar and steel but what he liked most
        was an eight foot post, the butt of a telephone pole.
Called it 'plantin' a deadman' for bobwire fence
        to stretch against. Made a hell'uva hole!

Big enough to bury a dog! Speakin' of which,
        last week he pitched straight over face down and died.
Not buildin' fence like you might think but on his knees
        tendin' trees that grew on the windbreak side.

For twenty years we neighbored well, which just makes sense,
        our common fence was always strong and tight.
But, Lord, he did things the hard way! Flat wore me out!
        But I don't doubt he tried to do'em right!

They struggled for an epitaph to consecrate,
        in words ornate, the place they'd lay his head.
They didn't ask me. I weren't no kin to the lad
        but if they had, this is what I'd said,

"He could sure set a post." One man's stand
        in the shifting sand of the world as it is today
That offered hope. An anchor, dug in deep,
        that helped to keep us all from driftin' away.

THE RANCHER AND THE BANKER

The rancher sat across the desk
  applying for a loan.
    He'd never borrowed cash before,
    he'd made it on his own.
But times were hard, as he explained
  and if they only could,
    He'd like to borrow twenty grand.
    The banker understood.

"That doesn't sound unreasonable,
  although it's quite a lot.
    Your cows can be collateral.
    How many cows you got?"
"Two hundred head," the rancher said,
  "That's give or take a few."
    "Well, that's enough," the banker said,
    "Of course there's interest due."

In three months time the rancher came
  and paid the loan in full
    But in his poke he had some left
    that was expendable.
"Why don't you leave that cash with me,"
  the banker said, content,
    "You put your money in my bank
    I'll pay ya eight percent."

The rancher paused, "Now let me see...
  you gave me twenty grand
    And then I paid you extra back
    for lendin' me a hand.
Now I give you this pile of cash
  and you pay me this time
    The extry that I done forked out,
    at slightly over prime?"

The banker nodded helpfully
  and lit himself a smoke.
    The rancher seemed to cogitate
    and then he finally spoke,
"I ain't too good at high finance...
  you've put me on the spot
    But fair is fair, so tell me, sir,
    how many cows you got?"

THE CALIFORNIA FARMER

The California farmer is possessed of a mystique
The rest of us sodbusters hold in awe and find unique

The abundance of their harvest, its variety and means
Is impressive to a farmer who grows corn and soybeans.

Now, it's not that we're not farmers in New York or Minnesota
But there ain't a sprig of artichoke in all of North Dakota!

Pistachios in Kansas and kiwis in Montana
Are scarcer than a fig tree in the state of Alabama.

And where did they get kumquats? Is broccoli Japanese?
And why do all their Holstein cows speak Dutch and Portuguese?

But California's bounty isn't all just Providence,
Some credit should be given to its early immigrants.

The California farmer has evolved since he began.
The land of milk and honey drew a simple kind of man.

They arrived with expectations in their worn out cars and boots,
They're amazed at their good fortune, they remember humble roots

'Cause they think that they're still dreamin', not sure it's gonna last
Like a starvin' cow that overnight is belly deep in grass.

So, in spite of their production and hi tech economics,
They're just like us, they mostly read the market and the comics.

Yup, the California farmer, when you turn up all the lights,
Ain't nothin' but an Okie with a loan and water rights!

COULD BE WORSE

The banker took his ledger out,
The rancher took a seat.
"Let's see, I lent you twenty thou
For cattle, corn and wheat.

"Let's talk about your cattle first."
The rancher's face looked pained.
"You know how bad the market's been,
Lost fifteen," he explained.

"Fifteen what! Fifteen cents a pound?
Fifteen died of thirst?"
"Nope, fifteen thousand dollars lost,
But, hey, it could be worse."

The banker swallowed hard then asked,
"Well, what about your grain?"
"The hoppers ate up all my wheat,
The sweet corn needed rain.

"The pig got sick. My son got drunk
And joined the Moonies' church!
I figger I'm down forty thou
But, hey, it could be worse!"

"Whataya mean, 'It could be worse!'
That ain't even funny!"
The rancher shrugged and then replied,
"Could'a been my money."

ALL BEEF NUGGETS

In the last twenty years there's been a significant trend toward larger cattle. Purebred breeders have concentrated their exotic genes 'til the modern bovine looks like a Great Dane on steroids! Our cattle have gotten bigger and bigger and bigger! It's gotten to the point where the Chianina people don't have to hire short Italians anymore to take that picture! But I'm wondering if maybe we're goin' the wrong way?

Maybe we should be breeding our cattle smaller and smaller and smaller . . . I'm talkin' BITE SIZE! Something that would fit in a hot dog bun or on a fondue stick! Convenience food!

Think how it would revolutionize our business. As producers, we wouldn't have to own all that land. We could give it back to the government. Turn everything into a prairie dog park. We could move into town, buy a nice house and turn our critters out in the backyard.

At branding time you wouldn't even have to furnish the banker with a horse. If he wants to count the cows just give him a grocery bag and point him out the back door. If you were cuttin' the bull calves you'd just reach into the grocery bag, pull out the calf, hold him in the palm of your hand and use your fingernail clippers!

And how 'bout hauling cattle? Look at their feet, cowboys, they were not meant to be off the ground! Nowhere in the Bible does it mention semi load! Say you wanted to haul your new mini-cattle to the sale or the stock show. You'd just put 'em in the back deck of the family car and go down the road. "Well, Mother, it's time to feed and water the stock." You whip into a Denny's, gather 'em up and turn 'em loose in the salad bar!

We'd put packin' houses outta business. Just clean 'em like a blue gill! Peel the hide off and eat 'em bone in! All beef nuggets!

There are some cowmen who have spent a lifetime improving their herd through genetic selection. They have made prodigious use of artificial insemination. There are actually people in our industry who have made a living artificially inseminating other people's cows! They are thinking to themselves as they read this, "Wait a minute! I can barely hit that deal the way it is now and you want me to...!" But I've got their problem solved too. Just dip 'em in it!

And finally, the greatest advantage of all is one we don't even think about. I read in the Wall Street Journal that folks are makin' a killin' today in microchips!

THE PHONE CALL

It's always been a mys'try
  In the winter when it's slow
Why a rancher gets up early
  When he's got no place to go!

He prowls around the kitchen
  Like a burglar on parole
In his air conditioned slippers
  With the toe there in the hole.

Then he builds a pot of coffee
  And has a little cup
'Til he thinks of some good reason
  To wake somebody up!

And all around the valley
  Folks are nestled in their bed
Unaware an egg is hatching
  In the rancher's little head.

He's reread the livestock paper
  Since getting up alone
But he's still not quite decided
  Just who he's gonna phone!

The assistant county agent?
  The forest ranger's boss?
The banker? Brand inspector?
  The commissioner that lost?

The vet? The Co-op salesman?
  Though he can't recall his name,
But it really doesn't matter
  'Cause anybody's game.

He quivers like a panther
  About to pounce his prey
As the innocent lay sleeping
  Just a dial tone away.

By daylight it's all over
  And he's reached a fever pitch!
The way he's stompin' 'round the house
  His wife is wond'rin' which

Potential victim got the call
  And had his brain massaged
With the lecture, she, just yesterday,
  Herself, had tried to dodge!

But little does she realize
  Just why he's in a tizzy,
See his neighbors got up earlier. . .
  And all the lines were busy!

ONE LAST LOOK

One last look at the rain gauge, the bottom's covered with dust.
One last look at the heavens. Can't see a cloud he can trust.

Far off sheets of heat lightning play tricks on the cowman's mind.
Bearing false witness they tease, leaving mirages behind.

"Good God! Don't it ever end!
I'm sick to death of this drought.
One more year like the last one
And I might as well sell out.

Hell, I've sold off half my cow herd
Still feedin' the others hay.
Nothin's green in the pasture,
I keep lookin' anyway.

I'm gettin' hard to live with,
'Specially with them that I love.
The Good Book teaches patience
But that, I'm runnin' short of.

So, I end up every evenin'
Out here on this little knoll
Checkin' the clouds for moisture
And, I guess, searchin' my soul

To keep me from forgettin'
That bad as it seems to be
The world's filled with people
That's a lot worse off than me.

Well, no point a'waitin' longer,
The sunset's cashin' it in.
Mother's makin' the gravy,
They'll wonder where I've been."

One last look at the rain gauge, filled to the brim with blue sky.
One last look at the heavens, must be a speck in his eye.

"Thy will be done," he whispers with a faith he can't explain.
But Lord, his faith would up some if "Thy will" included rain.

WORKIN' FER WAGES

I've worked fer wages all my life
   watchin' other people's stock
And the outfits I hired on to
   didn't make you punch a clock

Let you work until you finished!
   Like the feedlots in the fall,
When they'd roll them calves in on ya
   they'd jis' walk the fence and bawl.

We'd check the pens and pull the sick
   and push and treat and ride
Then process new arrivals
   that kept comin' like the tide.

And I've calved a lotta heifers
   though it's miserable sometimes,
It's somethin' that I'm good at
   and it's like she's sorta mine.

She knows I ain't the owner
   but we're not into protocol.
She's a cow and I'm a cowboy
   and I guess that says it all...

Got no truck with politicians
   who whine and criticize
'Bout corporate agribusiness,
   I guess they don't realize

Somebody's gotta own'em
   that can pay the entry fee!
Why, who they think puts up the dough
   to hire ol' boys like me?

Oh, I bought a set of heifers once
   maybe fifteen years ago.
I held'em through a calvin'
   then I had to let'em go

'Cause all I did was worry
   'bout how to pay the bills.
Took the fun outta cow punchin'.
   I don't need them kinda thrills.

Though I wouldn't mind a 'ownin' me
   a little hideaway
So when some outfit laid me off
   I'd have a place to stay.

But I figger I'm jis' lucky
   to be satisfied at heart
That I'm doin' what I'm good at
   and I'm playin' a small part

In a world that's complicated,
   where the bosses fight it out
With computers and consultants
   and their counterparts with clout.

They're so busy bein' bosses,
   they've no time to spare, somehow,
So they have to hire someone like me
   to go out and punch their cow.

KARL'S FIRST SALE

Anybody that has ever put on their own livestock sale knows Murphy's Law. Lew and Benny hired on to help Karl make his first purebred offering a success. Karl (that's Karl with a K) was a good cowman who did things the old way. Hard work was all he knew. Lew claimed he was the toughest man he ever met. He was oblivious to pain. He was that rare combination of brute strength and awkwardness. He didn't understand the fine points of creative financing or investor counselling. His neighbors even suggested that Karl was a little stupid. They were still sayin' it after their banks had foreclosed and they were doin' day work for Karl!

The day before the sale, it rained . . . and rained. They got the sale ring panels up, built the auction box and bleachers, and rented Porta Potties. They washed cattle, borrowed coffee makers, printed programs, bought ketchup, raked gravel and re-inforced the loading chute.

"Now, boys," says Karl, *"I like my cattle worked gentle and easy. No chousin'em! No need to cowboy here. Saddle up and follow me. We'll gather the bulls from across the road."*

As the bulls came outta the timber, they began to drift toward a fresh plowed field. They were frisky, kickin' up a little. Karl thought they were makin' a break for it . . . He panicked! *"Stop'em, boys!"* Karl charged the herd like Santa Anna takin' the Alamo! The bulls scattered into the knee deep mud like frightened quail! Karl raced across the field to head'em off. His horse shot through an open gate! A two-inch wide homemade strap-iron gate hinge reached out and tore a 15-stitch piece outta Karl's right ear! Never phased him!

Lew took a break from rewashin' the bulls. He heard poundin' and walked into the barn. Karl had his 17 foot extension ladder leaned against a 2X4 beam in the ceiling. Lew and Benny had nailed that beam lightly to the roof trusses from the bottom. The nails were heads down. Karl was hammerin' a light fixture into the top of the beam with all his might. Every resounding 'thwack' separated the beam further from the trusses. Karl was directly above Lew's Spring-O-Matic tilt table. The Spring-O-Matic had vertical pipes that stuck up like bamboo spears in a tiger trap!

Just as Lew raised a warning finger, a final hammer blow knocked the beam free! Beam, hammer, ladder, light fixture, bird's nest and Karl, plummeted into the Spring-O-Matic! When he rose from the wreckage, it looked like somebody had done a wheelie on his forehead!

Benny had jackknifed the feed wagon in the main entrance of the sale barn the night before, for easy access. *"Let's git that outta the way!"* said Karl. He jumped up in the tractor seat, jammed the ol' Farmall in 4th HIGH, blew the dust out the exhaust and popped the clutch! He dumped 4 tons of chopped straw in the doorway! The wind picked it up and piled it in Dakota drifts over the bleachers.

Sale day was crisp and cold. At Karl's suggestion, Lew and Benny drug a big smudge pot into the crowded sale barn. They lit it and turned it on HIGH. As long as it burned full blast it didn't smoke, but it sure put out the heat. Bidders were down to their tee shirts when the fuel finally ran out and it began to smoke. A black cloud settled over the straw-covered crowd.

Lew hooked a chain around the sizzling, smoking pot and pulled it out into the road. He went back to the cattle and worked until he heard the explosion! Rushing around the barn, he saw Karl laying flat on his back! His arms and legs were spread out like he was makin' gravel angels! His hat was blowed off and the front of his shirt looked like a barbecue grill! Lew thought he was dead!

The smudge pot had disappeared. Apparently Karl had gone out to refill the smudge pot with diesel. When he poured the fuel into the red-hot metal, it created fumes which ignited and turned the pot into a grenade! His wife covered Karl's face with Unguentine. His hat looked like he'd worn it to welding practice and he couldn't hear very well.

Back in the sale barn, the action was heating up. Don was the ring man. He'd backed up behind the corner of the auction box, because the bull that was sellin' was on the fight. Karl was settin' in the auction box intently watching the crowd. He was absent-mindedly switchin' the bull's nose with his whip popper. The bull began to shake and twitch. The more Karl diddled, the madder he got. Unable to take the torment any longer, the bull charged the auction box and lifted it three feet off the ground! The auctioneer fell backwards, spurs up, right outta the cockpit! Karl pitched forward into the sale ring!

The bull had him down and was grinding him into the sawdust! Don grabbed a metal folding chair and swung it at the bull! The bull swerved at the last second and Don blindsided Karl upside the head! Cold-cocked him! Karl went down like a bag of loose salt! There was a gash between his eyebrows and his off side ear looked like a gutted salmon! To this day Karl thinks it was the bull that got'im. Don's never told him different.

Benny walked up to Lew who was standin' in the sale ring door surveying the battlefield. "Sorry I got you into this, Benny, a man should get hazard pay workin' for Karl."

"Shoot," said Benny, "I'll work here next year for nothin' just to see what happens!"

THE SHOW RING JUDGE

The judge stood in the show ring as the yearlin' bulls arrived.
Noted and prestigious, his reputation had survived

A thousand purebred standoffs and a million county fairs
And despite his regal bearing, he didn't put on airs.

Oh, maybe just a little but nobody seemed to mind,
The purple robe and scepter made the show look more refined.

He stood straight with self assurance and whispered to his aide
As the bulls marched in a circle, years of breeding on parade.

It took him near an hour to arrange and classify
But he finally stood triumphant to explain his reasons why,

*"I've judged these shows for forty-odd years. The cycles come and they go.
They either get smaller or larger and I just roll with the flow.*

*I sort'em according to tallness. Their height from withers to claw.
I line'm up in that order, accounting for blemish or flaw,*

*Then I pick the size that is pop'lar and give that bull the high sign
And anything taller gets shuffled back to the end of the line!*

*It's a method that I've adopted that has set my mind at ease
And though it's often successful, not every purebred man agrees.*

*So, I allow for some dissention but like any Boy Scout
I always prepare for disaster . . . by knowin' the quickest way out!"*

THE FIELDMAN

There's a joke where the salesman points out
The swine feed in his catalogue
Will make'm grow faster, and the farmer
Answers, "So? What's time to a hog?"

The auction drug on, the auctioneer droned, the livestock were sellin' sky high.
The ringmen were wired, good fieldmen all, in a sports coat, white hat and tie.

They exhorted the buyers to rally contorting like cephalopods
While the crowd stared back, like Buddhas they sat, reluctantly giving their nods.

Each tip of the hat was met with a yell and a passionate pirouette
Bullying buyers to bid on the bull driving them deeper in debt!

"Say, how 'bout a sheep? They're great for the lawn!" *"Thanks anyway, got one last year."*
"Well, how 'bout a pig? They sure make good pets!" *"No thanks, got my own auctioneer!"*

Banging their programs, pacing like tigers they searched every face in the crowd
For some daring soul who'd give'm the eye, they were flaming, fireproof and loud!

"Git off yer duff! Git yer hands in the air! Look alive and stay on yer toes!
Cast yer eye on this cow! She's a dandy, even plays piano and sews!

"She's a vet'inarian's dream come true! She's never been pampered or brushed!
And listen to this. . . It's yer lucky day! She's open and ready to flush!"

Over and over and cow after cow the auction went on and time dragged.
The crowd was melting like tar in July, yet never a fieldman flagged!

The lady who sat with the auctioneer, though certainly no physician,
Got worried about the bid takin' boys and pointed out their condition,

"Those men in the ring are dead on their feet! They're exhausted, for Heaven's sake!
They've been at it for hours, workin' like dogs! Don't you think they're needin' a break!

The auctioneer was taken aback! He couldn't believe his ears!
He said, "The way these boys measure their time is in intervals between beers.

"It's pointless, I'm sure, to give'm a break 'cause they never have any plans.
It'd be like givin' a watch to a clock to keep track of the time on its hands!"

He scratched his head, perplexed by the notion and replied, "I don't understand?
It's nice yer concerned, but with all due respect, what's time to a fieldman?"

ARDEL'S BULL

Now Ardel's cows are all crossbred
   in the fullest sense of the word,
part Hereford, Holstein or Llama
   and maybe some Yak in the herd!

He had one ol' Bramer confusion
   whose hide was loose as a goose
with a hump that flapped like diaper
   and pendulous lips like a moose!

So, when he showed up at the bull sale
   we didn't expect him to buy
A genuine purebred herd sire.
   He wasn't that kind of a guy.

And we were right, least for a while
   'cause he never bid over eight.
The bulls were sellin' for twice that
   'til Lot Number 12 hit the gate.

He had an obvious defect
   that showed on the front of his face.
One eye was blue as a marble,
   the other stared out into space!

The bidding was apathetic.
   The buyers were quiet as mice.
So Ardel slid in like a coyote
   and bought him at hamburger price.

"Sold! Let him out, boys, he's finished!"
   We took one last look at the ox
Who stumbled over the sawdust
   then, bumped into the auctioneer's box!

"Dang it, Ardel! What's the story?"
   asked the ringman who stood by the door.
"Well," said Ardel, *"Not complainin',
   I'd'uv paid considerably more*

*"To improve my herd's genetics
   but, in truth, he's the best I could find.
See, my cows are so dadgum ugly
   I needed a bull that was blind!"*

THE CULL

"Hey, wait a minute, Wallace! Don't I recognize this cow?
Seems like we culled'er 'bout this time last fall."
"What cow? This cow?" "Yeah, the one here in the chute
whose foot looks like a ten pound cannonball!"

*"I don't b'lieve she's limpin' Doc. You can see that for yourself.
Besides, it makes her easier to track.
Plus she's bred."* **"How do you know?"** *"Because my brother checked her.
He can tell the way the hair lays on their back."*

"Oh, great! But what about this lump jaw and these patches where the hide
looks like somebody hit'er with a sander?"
*I'll have you know that lump jaw broke and drained two weeks ago.
and them patches? Well, what's a little dander."*

"Dang it, Wallace, yer not listenin'! Just look at this left eye.
It's scarred so bad she's prob'ly lost her sight."
*"Aw, Doc, that never worried me. Our ranch is big enough
she'd make it home if all she turned was right!"*

"There's Spanish moss a'hangin' on her antlers, she's so old.
Her brand looks like she's growed another hoof!"
*"Well, she ain't no show ring dandy. I never said she was.
She might be old but she's still waterproof."*

"I don't know why I bother. Yer stubborn as a mule.
You've got my best professional advice
Yet you've chosen to ignore it so now, for all I care
you can run'er 'til they're pavin' hell with ice!"

*"Oh, Doc, don't take it pers'nal. Just git yer plastic sleeve
and check'er, then we'll move on to another.
"Well?"* "I don't believe it... She's bred." *"Hey, Doc, don't take it hard.
You might could sell yer practice to my brother!"*

THE SQUEEZE CHUTE

The sun shone dull on its metal bars.
  The snow lay drifted against the frame.
Behind the barn near the rusting cars
  It's ended up all crippled and lame.

     An ol' squeeze chute I'd opened and closed
      On a hundred thousand heads and horns
     Dragged to the boneyard to decompose
      Forgotten rose in a bed of thorns

I lay my hand on the frozen steel,
  The head bar polished as smooth as glass.
The mem'ries flowed and the past revealed
  Itself like magic. I knew at last

     Why, through the years of sweat and toil,
      Despite the urge to romanticize,
     I hated it just like a boil
      That throbbed like the Starship Enterprise!

Its dinosaurial devious brain
  Laying in wait for liver and loin,
Slipped a ratchet and jiggled a chain
  Then rendered me a blow to the groin!

     It came to collect its pound of flesh.
      A finger here, there, a piece of shin.
     The aching ribs, recalling a'fresh
      A gleeful, scything crack to the chin!

Hot forged in hell by the River Styx.
  It's what they'd make if devils could weld!
They say machinery and cows don't mix
  And that truth has never been dispelled.

     But maybe I'm being too unkind.
      There's some that says she deserves a crown
     And, in fairness I could be inclined,
      As final tribute, to melt her down

And mold her into a plumber's snake.
  A generous way to salute'r,
And pay her homage, for ol' time's sake
  Everytime I called Roto Rooter!

GRAFTIN' CALVES

I was ugly when I was born. How ugly were you? I was so ugly they had to tie my mother's legs together so I could nurse! If you've ever grafted a calf you know just what I'm talkin' about.

In the old days when a cowman had a heifer that had lost her calf, he'd kick her out and let her heal up. He'd run her with the bull that spring and give her a second chance. Then . . . he sent his kid to ag school! She returned full of knowledge and explained to him that runnin' a cow without a calf is not a sound economic practice. The solution was to graft an orphan calf onto the heifer.

Not as easy as the Extension phamphlet might indicate! That heifer has learned through eons of evolutional instinct not to take something that is not hers. But, we're going to trick her!

Picture this heifer; she has just gone through the most traumatic period in her young life. She's exhausted, she weighs 750 pounds, her tailhead sticks up like a shark's fin and she's got a bag the size of a teacup! You go to town and come back with a 150 pound Holstein bull calf!

Ever since the time of Noah's Livestock Auction and Commission Company, peddlers have been offering magical formulae that guarantee the heifer will take the calf! Every cowman I know has a secret formula that worked for him once twenty years ago. He wants *you* to try it. Different scents abound: musk from a rutting beaver, compost drops, eucalyptus oil, Limburger lotion or grizzly after shave. They all have one thing in common, they smell like two dead carp in a Hefty trash bag on a warm Phoenix afternoon!

I've tried'em all. I even used the ol' sheepherders trick of skinnin' the dead calf and putting the hide on the live calf. A procedure that takes both of 'em off the best dressed list in the wink of an eye!

My most effective method uses a very subtle technique. One so delicate and difficult to describe, that it may be truly understood only by the most devout attender of horse training clinics. It is cow psychology at its finest. I call it . . . SHOVEL TRAINING!

You put the heifer and orphan calf in a small pen and hobble the heifer. The calf goes to suck, she kicks at him. You hit her with the shovel! A firm tap on the poll is preferred.

Soon all you have to do is stand outside the pen and display the shovel. The heifer freezes in place! Eventually the calf gets the idea. He recognizes the sound of your pickup comin' down to the calvin' barn. You start down the alley. He's got his head through the gate wavin' you on, "Down here! Bring the shovel!"

I don't know if this method works on mules, kangaroos or Congressional aides, but I'd recommend it for yer good ol' run of the mill black bally.

THE CATTAIL BOG

We see lots of cartoons about mechanized cowboys. The Lone Ranger on his three-wheeler, Tonto on a MoPed. Helicopters, snowmobiles, ATV's, jet boats and skateboards are all rumored to have been used handling cattle. Last month, Tom showed me photographic proof that Canadian cowboys are on the cutting edge of space-age buckaroodom.

The picture shows Tom sittin' on the hood of his ol' Chevy pickup. His feet are on the bumper and he's braced against the patented Osadczuk Roping Bosun's Chair and Dally Post. Delores, his long suffering, is shown behind the wheel (hands over her ears) as he guides her across the plains of Alberta on the heels of a cow in need of attention.

The next photo shows the cow roped and being cajoled into the stock trailer, parked nose to tail, on the far side of the pickup. Photo three shows Tom effusively thanking Delores for doing such a fine job helping him.

He said it worked slick as a whistle. I remember once when I could have used Tom's help. It was one of those cold spring days when the windbreak didn't cast a shadow. Eight hundred bred cows were scattered out on a half section of alfalfa stubble. They were calvin' right along with the usual smattering of trouble. I received an S.O.S. that morning but it was late in the day before I arrived to administer first aid.

Hank, the cowboy, said he had a cow with a dead calf in her. "She's out in the pasture," he told me. I bumped across the field in my vet truck while Hank accompanied me horseback. It was chilly but at least the ground was dry. Next thing I knew, Hank came flyin' over a hummock with that cow on the end of his 50-foot rope! She headed straight for a swamp of cattails, the only low spot for 20 miles. She did a half gainer and slid in on her side!

I waded into the ankle-deep water and began the unpleasant process of removing the dead calf. Encountering a slight hip lock, I took Hank's rope and looped it around the calf's middle.

"Give me a steady but gentle pull," I instructed Hank as he took a dally. I squatted behind the cow just as Hank's horse spooked, popped the calf out, drug the stinking carcass across my chest and knocked me flat on my back! The cow rolled over on my feet and squished me into the mud! Then she rose, dripping, and escaped.

I last saw Hank buckin' over the horizon, both hands on the horn, dragging' what was left of the unfortunate calf!

I drove the 80 miles home in my soggy boxer shorts. The heater was blowin' on my spindly legs and my sopping clothes lay on the pickup floor. I guess I should be thankful I wasn't stopped by the law. It was bad enough when I stopped off for coffee!

FETAL EYE VIEW

"Say, anybody got a light? It sure is dark in here
       and tighter'n the skin on Polish sausage.
For nine long months I've trusted Mom but now she's pulled the plug!
       A pure and simple case of double crossage!

I'm not sure what I really am or even what I'm for?
       To breed? Or do they plan to milluk us?
I've checked myself the best I could . . . a bull calf's what I think,
       but, heck, that might be my umbilicus!

Hey, close the door! I feel a draft, and git yer hands off me!
       Nobody said I had to relocate.
The way yer pawin' at my foot and pullin' on my leg
       you prob'ly never had a second date!

Oh, chains. That's nice. I guess this means the honeymoon is over.
       And I'd been counting on a baby shower
To celebrate my coming out, so you could lavish me
       with medicated gifts so I won't scour.

But, as it is, yer draggin' this hole project out too long.
       Yer midwife skills are lax and don't assure me.
Well don't stop now! Least let me git where I can turn my head!
       I'm feelin' like a piece of taxidermy!

Whoa! What's that pipe with all the hooks and evil lookin' leavers!
       You dummies plan on buildin' you a bridge?
Wait, don't tell me, let me guess . . . a fetal calf extractor
       for uterine abuse and pilferage.

Oh, way to go, now I'm hiplocked. Yer workin' up a sweat
       and smellin' like a pair of dirty socks.
I'm swingin' like a pendulum, what's that a'hangin' down . . . ?
       Is that my breakfast there between the hocks!

Git out the way! I'm bailin' out! Too bad we met like this
       'Cause you might be alright, at least, I think . . .
And to show there's no hard feelin's, belly up here to the bag
       and I'll buy you and all yer friends a drink!"

THE FEEDLOT MANAGER

Ah, the joys of upper management, of prestige and respect,
Making million dollar deals based on guts and intellect.
To co-ordinate production with disbursements every day,
His job, to run a feedlot and make that sucker pay!

    He arrives to work at daybreak and drives around the yard.
    Everything is peace and quiet, but his ulcer is on guard.
    He's wary, but sees nothing to disturb the morning still
    Then *WHOOMP!* From outta nowhere! An explosion at the mill!

The boiler's outta business! The welder's outta town!
But it doesn't make much difference 'cause the feed trucks 'er broke down!
So he clamors on the radio to get the cattle fed
But the feed boss is hungover and laid up home in bed.

    The mill's still raining shrapnel! The feed bay is a mess
    When the cattle foreman calls to say the calves are under stress.
    They're backed up at the squeeze chute, the hydraulic line froze tight!
    And could he send an ambulance, there's been a little fight!

Then his secretary tracks him down to say she's got the flu,
There's cattle in the neighbor's yard, his margin call is due.
She said down at the stackyard somebody's spotted smoke
And up in pen one-seventeen the waterline is broke!

    His wife called... from a public phone. Her car won't start again,
    The packer wants to wait a week to ship pens nine and ten.
    In his office waiting patiently's the Pro-Biotics man
    And a group of eager tourists on a field trip from Japan,

Plus the crew from 60 Minutes, his daughter's third grade class
And a roper needin' one day's work to buy a tank of gas.
So, one by one he handles it. He screams and shouts and squawks
And pours himself a double shot of Maalox on the rocks!

    Another day in management... another wooden horse.
    It's no wonder he's incapable of social intercourse.
    He's lived so long upon the razor's edge of the unknown
    That he's not allowed in public view without a chaperone!

Now standing in the shambles of a mornin' shot to hell
His youthful expectations are exposed and bid farewell
By the motto of a manager who knows he's in his prime
That says, "Though everything's okay...it's just a matter of time!"

THE CONSULTANT

Bein' in between jobs ain't no picnic.
  In fact, it's downright insultant.
  So I printed some cards, put signs in the yard,
  And bingo, became a consultant!

I solicited quality rest stops
  In search of the right clientele.
  Passed out ballpoint pens to all of my friends,
  Got an answer machine from Ma Bell.

At last an ol' timer sought my advice.
  He brought in his last balance sheet.
  I saw with a smile his management style
  Was outdated and obsolete.

So I set out to solve all his problems.
  I spoke like a preacher possessed!
  He sat there amazed, his eyes sorta glazed,
  I could see he was truly impressed.

He said not a word as I rambled on.
  For effect, I went over it twice.
  When time had expired, he politely inquired,
  "How much for this expert advice?"

I said, "Fifty bucks." I thought it was fair.
  From his looks I thought I could fake it.
  But he nodded his head and finally said,
  "Well, son, I don't think I'll take it!"

THE CONSULTING NUTRITIONIST

In the 20th Century world of feedlots there is a person who combines the qualities of Albert Einstein, Charles "Call me Chuck" Amway and Dr. Joyce Brothers. A person who possesses intellect beyond the understanding of simple laymen, who can sell tallow to a vegetarian evangelist, and is able to convince a feedlot manager that life is worth living after $1.16 feeders and eight dollar corn! Yes friends, the Consulting Nutritionist!

Able to read feed bunks from a Cessna at 5,000 feet, able to analyze rations from the desk of an air conditioned office and able to evaluate performance by reading the tea leaves on a meringue cow pie, the Consulting Nutritionist stands ready to aid the feedlot manager in his fight against pore doers!

Armed with a cellular phone and a computer that plugs into the cigarette lighter, they make their appointed rounds. Always stopping first at the manager's office for the obligatory counselling session, then driving down the alleys, brow furrowed, lot sheet in hand, peering eye level at those contented bovine at the bunk. Then back to the office to return sixteen phone calls, lunch with the management and down the road.

I used to watch as they circled the feedyard, waving a finger at the occasional cowboy, pen cleaner or truck driver. I would be buried in sick calves, dried blood to the elbow and 50% Dextrose dribbling down my arm.

'I'm a professional, too', I would think as I plunged a caked thermometer up a cocci calf, smearing the right side of my covies with fetid feces, *'Why don't they ever ask me to lunch?'*

Jealous? Yes. Maybe I was envious of the seemingly exalted position Consulting Nutritionists enjoy in feedlot work.

Dr. Miles DVM was called to the feedlot to examine several steers who had apparently died of bloat, all in the same pen! Obviously a feed problem.

Similarly alerted, the Consulting Nutritionist arrived, drove to the pen and rolled down his power window. He counted the necropsied carcasses and remarked, **"Do ya think after six yer convinced it's bloat?"**

Dr. Miles waved away the flies and answered, **"You wanna post the other six to see fer yerself?"**

The nutritionist studied him a minute, gave him a look of disdain, powered up his window and drove off.

Doc turned to the cowboy helpin' him and said, *"Ya know, when they invented electric windows they reduced the nutritionist's work load by 50%!"*

PILED HIGHER AND DEEPER

Ol' Bubber was cussin' his bad luck
As we watched his bunch crossin' the scale.
Which surprised me a bit 'cause he had to admit
His steers were the best at the sale!
      Weighed eight fifty-two . . . after truckin'!
      Which puzzled me some, I confess.
      My quandry, ya see . . . he was neighbors to me
      And mine weighed considerably less!
But still he appeared dissappointed.
He spoke as he stared at the floor,
"I can't understand, as hard as I planned
Why them steers didn't weigh a lot more.
      See, A & M put on a meeting.
      Extension was all out in force.
      I needed to change how I handled my range
      And they had the answers, of course!
Brush hog the greasewood, burn all the pear,
And fly on the N, P and K.
By killin' my weeds and plantin' their seeds
My gains would get better each day.
      Merlin the Nutritionist spoke of
      Ionophores and methanol gas.
      He had a few tricks like trace mineral mix
      So they'd weigh more comin' off grass.
Then the supplement salesman added
It all could be fed in his feed.
It showed on his graph a pound and a half
Was expected, and Merlin agreed!
      The vet told me BVD cattle
      Gained less and I should vaccinate
      It was all Greek to me but HE had a degree
      And Lord knows I needed the weight!
Ear tags improved their performance
So I spent another big wad.
The message was clear, I put five in each ear
And even hung one on the cod!
      Then the implant peddlers attacked me!
      Convinced me my work wasn't done!
      I had to agree so I used all three
      Heck they even threw in a gun!
Then Alan Savory told me
What he'd learned out on the Savannah.
Ignoring expense, I bought enough fence
To hot wire the state of Montana!
      I wormed'em, dehorned'em and dipped'em
      I sprayed'em . . . hell, I did it all!
      Group therapy sessions, a priest for confessions
      And even a heifer on call!
So you see, I took ALL their advice!
I was baffled by brilliance galore.
And my steers did okay but I's hopin' that they
Would have weighed considerably more.
      'Cause if BS was measured in light bulbs
      My steers should have lit up the town
      And shown like a beacon, synergistically speakin'
      And weighed over two thousand pounds!"

THERIOGENOLOGIST

Theriogenologist? I was one and didn't even know it! A specialist in animal reproduction. An ovary observer, a diddler of the zygote. One who has devoted his life to preserving pregnancy...a cow plumber.

Included in this broad field are embryo transplanters, diagnostic palpaters, infertility detectives, fertility evaluators, artificial inseminators and others identified by their green fingernails and white socks.

Those folks who practice this profession are an unusual group. They don't wear a tie to work. They approach their business like a professional football player, knowing when the game's over they're gonna look a lot worse. It is not a career for the fastidious.

Genghis Khan or Attila the Hun would have been good theriogenologists. However, Fred Astaire or Mr. Rogers might feel ill at ease in a pair of muddy five-buckle overshoes with manure in their ear. They would make better equine practitioners.

People who work at the rear end of a cow develop a similar personality. They're usually "good ol' boy" types who have a high humiliation level. If one were easily embarrassed, under a cow's tail, behind the gun so to speak, is not the place to be.

There are dangers. Like the veterinarian who was preg checking one fine afternoon when the cow went down in the chute, breaking his arm. The fractured bone pierced his plastic sleeve and lodged him securely inside the cow like a fishhook.

But most injuries are more damaging to one's self esteem. Like Gary, a struggling newlywed who was doing artificial insemination to enhance his meager graduate student income. He arrived at the dairy with only one plastic sleeve in his kit. It lasted for five cows. Gritting his teeth he approached cow number 6 and palpated her bare-handed. Gruesome perhaps, to the non-cowperson, but an accepted alternative to the dedicated theriogenologist. As he began his treasure hunt in the final cow he must have said something "unprofessional" because she kicked him on the inside of the thigh! He was elbow deep in Holstein at the time. She clamped down on his arm as he fell to the ground writhing in pain.

Driving home that evening in stinking agony he made a terrifying discovery. He had lost his untarnished, two month-old, 24 karat, 5 year payment plan, once in a lifetime extravagance, diamond studded wedding ring ... inside the cow!

Next morning he returned to the dairy armed with a metal detector and was seen for days wandering through the fields, going from patty to patty like a beachcomber high on propane fumes.

The bride was not happy. The mother-in-law was vindicated, however, since she had warned her daughter not to marry someone who makes a living that no one can pronounce.

THE #2 HAIRBALL

Ever buy one of those feeders
  That never seems to get well?
    Right off the truck to the sick pen
      Straight from Receiving to hell!

They're common. Each semi load's got one
  'Specially if they're from a sale.
    I call'em a Number 2 Hairball,
      They're fluffy, but thin as a rail.

They look like those two day old cornflakes
  That stick to the side of the bowl.
    Pot bellied, wormy and drippin'
      From every unplugable hole.

His muzzle's as wide as a suitcase,
  His tail comes down to his heels,
    His hide's as dry as a Baptist bar,
      The last brand still hasn't peeled!

You treat'em for weeks with your potions
  With everything Doc recommends
    But sixty days later he still gets his mail
      Addressed to the hospital pen.

Where do these chronics all come from?
  I've had some time to reflect.
    There's a purebred herd of 'em somewhere . . .
      At least that's what I suspect.

A place where animal science
  And Doctor Frankenstein meet.
    Where the characteristics they breed for
      Are the same ones you try to treat!

Like, only one lung ever works right.
  The cough's just part of the deal
    And scours is standard equipment
      Plus the footrot that never will heal.

No matter which treatment you try out
  You're confused at every attempt.
    'Cause one hundred four point seven
      Is really their normal temp!

So you keep pumpin' medicine in'em
  'Til the drug bill is high as the sky
    Yet they never completely recover
      But the bloody buggers won't die!

Now, of course, I'm makin' this all up.
  No chronic cow breeder's been caught.
    But if I was a medicine maker. . .
      I just might give it some thought.

KEEP ON TRUCKIN'

Horses were meant to be ridden
Chickens were meant to be fried
Fish were meant to be cat food
Pigs were meant to be styed
Sheep were meant to be sweaters
Eagles were meant to be bald
But never, and I mean never, my friend,
Were cattle meant to be hauled!

Pintos were meant to be spotted
Zebras were meant to be striped
Plants were meant to be potted
Menudo was meant to be triped
Foxes were meant to be clever
Scrimshaw was meant to be scrawled
But never, and I mean never, my friend,
Were cattle meant to be hauled!

Clams were meant to be chowdered
Puppies were meant to be wormed
Turkeys were meant to be gobbled
Poodles were meant to be permed
Skeeters were meant to be swatted
Ducks were meant to be called
But never, and I mean never, my friend,
Were cattle meant to be hauled!

Frogs were meant to be princes
Lions were meant to be king
Salads were meant to be Waldorf
Vases were meant to be Ming
Poems were meant to be ended
Lang Syne was meant to be Auld
But never, and I mean never, my friend,
Were cattle meant to be hauled!

No Shirt, No Service
No sudden moves
And last of all
No cloven hooves!

THE MARKER

The very first time I saw him, he was comin' off the truck.
  The order buyer had averaged down, or else just plain got stuck!
  He went in a pen of feeders but when it came time to sell
  The packer buyer cut him off. The reason was plain as hell,

'Cause he looked like a long haired Jersey! At least he did to me
  And there might have been a camel somewhere in his family tree
  'Cause he'd shed his hair in patches, past the point of no return
  Sorta like a shaggy carpet that somebody'd tried to burn!

So, he went with tailenders and got sorted off again
  And made the rounds when springtime came just goin' from pen to pen.
  That summer he went out to grass but he never gained a pound,
  We vaccinated him that fall on his second time around.

The weeks drug on but I kept track, in truth he was hard to miss,
  'Cause he stuck out like a cold sore on the lips you'd planned to kiss!
  One day I told the foreman, *"Ya know, ol' Red's been here a while,
  I've figgered his performance up and it's time to reconcile."*

I had calculated that he'd had six hundred days on feed.
  Been through the chute so many times he was almost broke to lead!
  He had eaten sixteen thousand pounds of grain since he'd begun
  And converted at a ratio of Two-Oh-Two to One.

Which, in fact, is pretty sorry, unless you're raisin' whale,
  So, that mornin' on the One-Ton, ol' Red got shipped to the sale.
  I was braggin' at the horse barn how I'd prob'ly get a raise
  For pointing out that keepin' poor producers seldom pays.

Some of the boys objected, but sentiment has no place
  In hard core ag economics. Red was a classical case.
  The foreman cut my lecture short that evenin' just about five,
  "Git yer butt down to Receiving . . . Time for the trucks to arrive."

New cattle were comin' from auctions, local and countrywide.
  When I went down to unload'em, I dang near laid down and cried!
  Ol' Red come strollin' off the truck like Caesar entering Rome.
  He gimme sort of a "Gotcha" look and said "Hi, Honey, I'm Home!"

THE FALL RUN

I was ridin' pens for Horton in the fall of '91.
It was early in October and the run had just begun.
He was buyin' calves like crazy 'cause the price was on the rise
And you couldn't see his pupils for the glitter in his eyes!

He bought big ol' soggy weaners . . . soaked up virus like a sponge!
He bought dime-off little leppies when the market made a lunge,
He bought Terramycin junkies that had been around the world
And hungry auction refugees that stuffed their cheeks like squirrels!

He bought growers offa wheatgrass, bought high mountain pasture calves,
He bought cuttin' bulls and ropin' steers, the have-nots and the haves,
Bought heifers that were baggin' up raised on leafy spurge and sage
And some that weighed two-fifty that were legal drinkin' age!

They were comin' in in boatloads! Trucks were backed up gunwale deep
'Til the nightman up and quit us 'cause they wouldn't let him sleep!
It was busy as an anthill at Receiving every day,
Calves were standin' in the alley, in the bunk and in the way!

All awaiting to be processed by the ragged cowboy crew
Who'd begun to look like prisoners doin' hard time at the zoo!
I was horseback checkin' new ones on the day before they broke
When the boss came drivin' up the bunk. He stopped and lit a smoke,

Took a Tums and shot of Maalox, blew his nose and spoke right out,
"Yessir, son," he said, *"This here's what cattle feedin's all about!"*
It was several days before I chanced to see him after that
'Cause all hell broke loose next mornin'! I was in up to my hat!

It was more than just an isolated outbreak in the yard.
Any good luck we had goin' was completely au revoired!
Even "wreck" would understate it. Catastrophic comes to mind.
Like a hurricane, a bad divorce and toothache intertwined!

A four-alarm tub chopper fire! A dose of gas gangrene!
Then topped off with a napalm strike and scabies quarantine!
Chicken Little should'a been there! He'da dang sure pooped his nest!
Every cowboy rode and doctored hardly gettin' any rest.

You can bet we earned our wages, kissed our one day off goodbye,
Workin' six o'clock 'til midnight, eatin' supper on the fly
'Til at last the plague just petered out . . . got gnawed down to the rind
And we've all got back to normal, 'cept the boss, who's now confined,

He's been checked into a clinic where they put'im every year
To recover and rejuvenate and let his conscience clear.
Sort of, Jiffy Lube for managers who've lost their sense of place
Where they git their eyes reglittered and their memory erased!

A LOVE STORY

This is a love story.

In a small ranching community in the west there lived a man, his wife and four children. They were no different than their neighbors. They ran cows, built fence and did their part to keep their little town alive.

The children attended the local school. Students numbered less than a hundred. But the remoteness of the area instilled a strong interdependence among the ranchers, families and townies.

The man and his wife lived in his folks' old house on the ranch. They planned to remodel someday but the vagaries of the cattle business, the demand for routine ranch improvements and the appetite of four teenagers combined to prevent any real home improvements.

When the youngest son began high school, the man dared to dream of the future. One where his wife could quit her town job and he could spend more time with her. For even after twenty years he never tired of her company.

Cancer, the assassin, drew down and shot out the light of his life.

His grief was deep. The community put their arms around this proud man and his family. They did what neighbors do. As the months passed, they were always there. Watching after his children while loneliness ground away at his broken heart. They watched over him, as well.

The fall that his youngest began his senior year the man sold his cow herd. The market was good and his interest in the ranch had waned.

One day I got a phone call from him. He introduced himself and invited me to speak at this son's graduation. I didn't recognize the name of the town. He said there were six in the graduating class.

Arrangements were made. He sponsored a big BBQ that afternoon. Four hundred attended. He took a few moments before my introduction at commencement that evening to address the crowd. I was unaware of his tragedy. He spoke simply but expressed his appreciation to his friends and neighbors. He never mentioned his loss. It was unnecessary. In a community like this, everyone knew.

Afterward some of us gathered in his living room for a nightcap. A few friends, his four kids, he and I. It was comfortable. The new graduate opened his gifts and spoke of his plans with the conviction and anxiety of youth. Nobody asked the man about his plans but you could hear the page turning in his life.

I guess the hand lettered sign hangin' on his gate post
out by the road said it all,

YAHOO! The last one finally graduated!

Thanks friends. **RANCH FOR SALE**

134

DADDY'S RANCH

I'm sittin' here at my daddy's old desk
  Just starin' out at the yard.
The barn looks the same as it always has,
  I guess that's why it's so hard.

    I can't put my finger on when it changed.
      When you come back every year
    You don't seem to notice that edges get round
      And yer footprints disappear.

Machinery that once roamed this furrowed ground's
  Evolved into dinosaurs.
The harness hangs empty, weary with age,
  Cobwebs have covered the doors.

    The fences are melting into the earth,
      The trees are sixty feet tall
    And here I sit in the afternoon sun
      Tryin' my best not to bawl

'Cause here in my hand's an overdue note
  With a letter in reply
You wrote him, Daddy, misspellings and all,
  Beggin' more time to comply.

    And another, a whole box full of bills.
      You're mortgaged up to the hilt!
    A slave's what you were! Indentured and tied
      To everything that you built

And you never said a word. All those times
  Whenever we talked on the phone
Just, "How's the kids? Yep, yer Mama's okay,"
  You had to do it alone.

    Too proud? Too stubborn? Too afraid? I think
      In the end it broke your heart.
    If only you'd told me, I could have helped,
      We'd gladly have done our part

To save the ranch. But as late as last week
  We talked, You said things were fine.
The lawyer went over your books today. . .
  'Sell out' was the bottom line.

    I know why you did it. Too well I know.
      To protect Mother and me.
    I love the ranch, but this ranch is nothin'
      Compared to you, don't you see.

You were my rock. And you always have been.
  In my mind you hung the moon
And now when I need you the most, you're gone,
  Oh, Daddy, you died too soon.

THE FARMER AND THE SALESMAN

"Don't be leanin' on my fender,"
said the farmer to the rep.
Take a look at this new seed corn,"
"Git yer foot offa my step!"

"And I've got a line of cleansers
to reduce your Bac-T count,"
"And reduce my line of credit
by the very same amount!"

"Not to mention scours vaccine
to prevent the dreaded crud,
and this iron enriched injection
to rejuvenate tired blood."

"I don't need yer blamed concoctions!
All my calves are at their peak!"
"Yeah, I noticed that yer deadman's pile
is smaller than last week,

And yer pigs are doin' better
since you bought my supplement."
"It's that parsley I been addin',
Not yer feed that makes 'em grunt!"

"How's that herbicide I sold ya?
Killed the weeds in yonder field."
"Huh! It rained just right this summer,
That's what doubled up my yield!"

"Do ya need some more inflations,
baler twine or rubber boots?"
"Read my lips! No milk replacer,
No organic substitutes!

Everything you try to sell me
Just adds to my expenses.
It's hard enough to keep'er
Runnin' smooth between the fences!

Can't you see yer takin' up my time.
I've got to go and feed.
So why don't you just up and leave . . .
What you think I'm gonna need."

THE PRACTITIONER'S LOT

Today in the world of modern vets
I've lost my place in line
My colleagues have prospered as specialists
In therio or swine.

I see their achievements in magazines,
Their articles in print.
They've developed a cure for seedy warts
With after dinner mints

Or they're recognized as the final word
In matters so complex
That I can't pronounce what they're working on
Much less, what it affects!

I spend my days at the back of a cow
Usually up to my chin
In the process of pullin' somethin' out
Or pushin' it back in!

Or I'm tryin' to pass a catheter
To move a calculi
While the cat is tearin' my arm to shreds
And sprayin' my good tie!

I dream to discover a new technique
But it's not meant to be.
The chances are slim that they'd even name
A prolapse after me!

But I'm thankful I've got a good practice
With loyal clientele
Who, in spite of my vast shortcomings, still
Try and speak of me well.

Why, just last week two farmers were talkin'
Outside my clinic door
"Doc ain't perfect, but for our little town
We couldn't ask for more."

"Yea, I'll agree," the second one answered,
"I've given it some thought,
With Doc you always git yer money's worth
But...he don't charge a lot!"

BARNEY OLDFIELD DVM

I think the only reason Jerry decided to become a veterinarian was so he could drive fast.

He took special pride in his vet truck, even souped up the engine and chromed the exhaust.

Realizing the importance of the vet in a rural community, the local constables often looked the other way when Doc passed them on a dusty two-lane at Mach 5!

Sunday morning, after early church, Jerry went down to his clinic, accompanied by his young son.

It was usually peaceful on Sunday mornings. He made his rounds and checked his patients. Back in the big pen, he noticed that one old cow had not survived his treatment... all four legs were pointing skyward.

He backed his rig into the pen, hooked onto her with a length of log chain and pulled her 'round to the leeward side of the clinic, where the dead man collected mistakes.

Just then, Jerry saw a trailer pull up front.

He jumped out of his rig and went to meet the client. As the morning wore on, emergencies continued to clock in. By 12:30 p.m., they were cleanin' up and plannin' to head home for Sunday's roast beef dinner, which his wife served promptly at 1 p.m.

At a quarter to, the phone rang. "Doc," said the caller, "I've got a prolapse in need of fixin'. I've already got'er in the trailer. Can I bring'er in?"

It was three o'clock when Doc and Jimmy finally headed for home. At the first intersection, Doc goosed his Chariot and turned left in front of a semi. The truck driver hit his air horn, but Doc cleared him by a car length!

He built up speed on the straight away, but something didn't seem right? The engine sounded good but it was luggin'. He slowed down to 60 and stomped on the gas.

The twin four-barrels kicked in and the G Force pushed him back in his seat! At 70 mph, he could still sense some aerodynamic impediment. Jerry knew his truck like the H and C in his shower; he should have been doin' 85!

He cruised into town. At the corner of 20th and Main, he stopped at the light. "Must be the dang emission control," he muttered to himself.

"Daddy, Look!" pointed Jimmy, "There's a cow in the road!"

Jerry craned around. Sure enough, there *was* a cow in the road. She looked familiar. She was attached to his pickup by 20' of log chain!

I asked him later if she was skint up pretty good.

"Not really," he answered, "I don't think she hit the ground that often!"

THE VET'INARY'S LAUNDRY

There is nothing more disgusting, more deserving to condemn
Than a basket full of laundry from the local D.V.M.!

See, afterbirth is oil base and needs to soak in hot
Like adiposal tissue but blood, of course, is not.

It requires a frigid bath to make the stain repent
Problem with cold water is it sets the tag cement.

Cat hair slips unnoticed even by the sharpest eyer
Then spreads like dying dandelions in contact with the dryer.

Samples long forgotten in pockets pasted shut
Flavor all the laundry with fermented porcine gut.

Organophosphate fragrance gently lingers in the air
Mixing with the rumen contents on his underwear.

Iodine and methyl blue, fetotomy remains,
Dog shampoo, dehorning paste and suppurating drains,

Abscessed ears and hooves and horns and poop from who knows what!
All gather in the dirty clothes to spot and clot and rot

And later gets recycled as that ever present scum
That's now part of your Maytag living on ad nauseum.

The vet'inary's laundry can disrupt a married life.
It's enough to make you jealous of a truck mechanic's wife!

But there is no lofty moral just a sense of deja vu,
A warning now remembered, that should have been a clue,

When your groom gave you his hanky as his darling bride-to-be,
You should have been suspicious when it smelled like tomcat pee!

So don't let bloody coveralls or body parts of cows
Distract you from the promise spoken in your wedding vows.

If laundry's come between you I'd suggest this little trick,
Soak the spots in gasoline and flick it with your BIC!

THE BANKER'S NIGHTMARE

This letter came owin' the postage down at the Mercantile Bank

Dear Sir,
>I received your inquiry
>>And I intend to be frank.
>
>My husband was laid off construction
>>When we applied for the loan.
>He planned to buy cows and get wealthy
>>But the man's accident prone!
>
>Enclosed is a check for the live ones,
>>Sold every cow we could find!
>I'm sending this detailed accounting
>>Forthwith, to settle your mind.
>
>The death loss played hell with the profit
>>But it kept my husband aroused.
>Why you lent that fool money, I'm stymied.
>>He don't know sic'cum 'bout cows!
>
>The first ol' bag died on arrival.
>>Never got off of the truck.
>We suspect five died of grass tetany
>>But, hell, who'd know with our luck!
>
>Then two of 'em died, calvin' problems
>>Or very soon after that.
>He backed over one with the tractor,
>>Nearly ran over the cat!
>
>And one of 'em fell down the creek bank,
>>He choked one dead in the chute,
>One escaped and died on the highway
>>Hit by the cop in pursuit!
>
>There's still two at large in the cedars,
>>Not much, a couple of snides.
>If we can't get'em caught by Friday
>>We'll shoot'em, bring in the hides.
>
>I'm not sure if there were more losses
>>Murphy's Law just ran its course
>But your note came due at a bad time,
>>Last week I filed for divorce.
>
>But don't give up hope on the balance
>>'Cause all of his ships ain't sank.
>The bum's got a job... makin' ag loans
>>At your competitor's bank!

144

THE PERFECT GIFT

For that certain special someone whose talent lays well hidden,
        Disguised as *barking spiders*, and often waits unbidden
Until it's least expected then, without a warning flings
        Its flatulent crescendo on sulfur scented wings.

What can you give a person with such windy expertise?
        A tuning fork? Some Chapstick? A metered time-release?
All ideas with some merit, but may I suggest a pair
        Of the latest thing in undies . . . I call it THUNDERWEAR!

It has acoustic panels to enhance, yet not disturb
        The resonant profundo when you activate reverb.
With practice you can dampen those explosive sharp reports
        Or by turning up the echo you can yodel through your shorts!

You can imitate a bugling elk, an octopus escape,
        Or counterpoint percussion with a Kenny Rogers tape.
Be a foghorn when it's needed, play a tasteful oboe lick
        Or recreate an ocean storm complete with Moby . . .

But you say he doesn't need it! He might hurt himself, you fear
        But it has its own extinguisher should he flame out while in gear
And to top it off it comes equipped, as per the O.S.H.A. warnings,
        With protective ankle splash guards for those jalapeño mornings!

And when he wakes and stumbles from your bed at break of dawn
        And tunes up like an orchestra awaiting the baton,
He can welcome in the morning with a twenty gun salute
        Or play his reeking bagpipe 'til he's just too pooped to toot!

I know yer thinkin', "I don't know . . . a duck call would be cheaper . . .'
        But in searching for the perfect gift, one digs a little deeper,
And the icing is this THUNDERWEAR is guaranteed to last
        Until his sphincter catches fire or he just runs outta gas!

JUST FRIENDS

I can't remember his number.
  I don't call him often enough.
His birthday alway escapes me
   'cause I don't keep up with that stuff.

  And I'm lucky if I see him
    even once or twice a year
  But I'm really not complainin'
    'cause we're still close, we're just not near.

I recognize his daughter's voice.
  I remember when she was born.
I was there when he got married!
  I held the ring his wife has worn

  For all these years, his darlin'.
    Ya know, she hasn't changed a bit.
  And him and me? We're markin' time
    by the bad habits that we quit.

Together we're ambidextrous!
  Although we're really not a pair
We've got each other covered
  and, between us, a full head of hair!

  We're part of each other's gristle,
    as inveterate as bone.
  It's nice how life can fix it
    so you don't have to go it alone.

As I sit here blowin' smoke rings
  from the pipedreams that I've had,
I'm wonderin' if I've told him
  how many times it's made me glad

  Just to know he's out there somewhere,
    like a dollar in my shoe,
  And how much it would please me
    if he felt the same way, too.

When I add up all my assets,
  he's one thing I can't appraise.
What's a promise or a handshake
  or a phone call worth these days?

  It's a credit with no limit,
    it's a debt that never ends
  And I'll owe him 'til forever
    'cause you can't be more than friends.

COWBOY CAMP CHRISTMAS

It was Christmas Eve at daybreak when we found him in the yard.
   His horse was porcupined with frost, the ground was frozen hard.
He must'a drifted in last night after we'd all gone to bed
   And had a fatal heart attack, 'cause, fer dang sure he was dead!
We recognized him right away as Tater Jack, the preacher,
   A fire and brimstone hard-nosed man, with one redeeming feature

He believed! And took it on himself to spread the Holy Gospel
   In places where the reg'lar church had deemed it near impos'ble.
We got to see him twice a year 'cause we wuz out a'ways.
   He usually came by Christmas and he'd stay a couple days.
Now, Christmas in a cowboy camp's a pretty lonely place
   And folks like us, that live alone, build a sorta carapace

Like turtles have. Which insulates our heart from too much feelin'.
   But Tater Jack cut no one slack! He preached like thunder pealin'!
And got right down to the question . . . What did Christmas really mean!
   Was it just another winter day to ply the old routine?
He'd dump the whole load on us, but what the heck, we had the time
   And he *was* a grand diversion. Thumpin' Bibles ain't a crime.

But he'd end each Christmas sermon with the passages from Luke.
   He explained, we were the shepherds . . . which he meant as no rebuke,
Then he'd traipse us all out in the dark and point straight up and say,
   "Fear not, I bring good tidings, Unto you is born this day
A Saviour, who is Christ the Lord! See them stars and us below . . .
   They were shinin' on them shepherds then, two thousand years ago!

So ya see, that's how it started, with a bunch of guys like you
   Who could see through all the hoopelah and give this day its due.
That's why He told the shepherds first. See, God trusts a simple man.
   So He signed yer kind up early 'cause He knew you'd understand."
Well, Tater Jack would ramble on but what he said held water
   And it made us cowboys kinda proud, and humble, like it ought'er.

Sam would play his ukelele and we'd sing a song or two
   I reckon we were better men 'cause ol' Tater'd drifted through.
So findin' him this mornin' put a damper on the day.
   We thawed him out and combed his hair and stored his stuff away.
Then buried him this afternoon, on his final Christmas Eve.
   We've all been sorta aimless since, maybe just too numb to grieve.

Russell Don had shot a sage hen and we saved it for tonight
   It was good, and we sure ate it all . . . but Christmas ain't quite right.
Tater Jack made it official, a snubbin' post to tie to.
   He gave Christmas real meaning. So, maybe we should try to
Carry on, like he would have us. Ain't none of us a preacher
   But no line camp bunch of cowboys ever had a better teacher,

"Sam, if you can play Hark the Herald Angels on your uke,
   I'll try and read the cowboy part . . . in those passages from Luke."

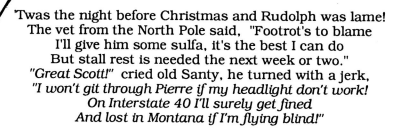

RUDOLPH'S NIGHT OFF

'Twas the night before Christmas and Rudolph was lame!
The vet from the North Pole said, "Footrot's to blame
I'll give him some sulfa, it's the best I can do
But stall rest is needed the next week or two."
"Great Scott!" cried old Santy, he turned with a jerk,
"I won't git through Pierre if my headlight don't work!
On Interstate 40 I'll surely get fined
And lost in Montana if I'm flying blind!"

"No cop in his right mind would give any clout
To a geezer who claimed that his reindeer went out!"
He gathered the others, ol' Donner and Blitzen,
Were any among'em whose nose was transmitzen?
They grunted and strained and sure made a mess
But no noses glowed brightly or ears luminesced.
"It's bad luck in bunches," cried Santy, distressed,
"We'll fly Continental, the Red Eye Express!

"I'll just check the schedule," he put on his glasses
When up stepped ol' Billy, the goat from Lampasas.
He shivered and shook like a mouse on the Ark
But his horns were a beacon...They glowed in the dark!
Santy went crazy! He asked *"Why?"* with a smile
"I just ate a watch with a radium dial!
Where I come from in Texas we don't have thick hide
My skin is so thin it shines through from inside."

"If that's true then let's feed him!" cried Santy with glee
"Gather everything burnin' and bring it to me!"
So Billy ate flashbulbs and solar collectors,
Electrical eels and road sign reflectors,
Firecracker sparklers, a Lady Schick shaver
And Lifesavers, all of em' wintergreen flavor,
Jelly from phosphorescellous fish,
Day Glow pizza in a glittering dish,

Fireflies and candles and stuff that ignites,
Then had him a big bowl of Northering Lights!
He danced on the rug and petted the cat
And after he'd finished and done all of that
To store up the static 'lectricity better
They forced him to eat two balloons and a sweater!
Then he opened his mouth, light fell on the floor
Like the fridge light comes on when you open the door!

His Halloween smile couldn't be better drawn
When he burped accidently, his high beams kicked on!
"Hitch him up!" cried ol'Santy, and they went on their way.
I remember that Christmas to this very day,
The sky was ablaze with the stars shining bright.
They were shooting and falling all through the night.
And I realize now, though my fingers are crossed
What I really was seein'...was ol' Billy's exhaust!

A COWBOY CHRISTMAS CAROL

This is the story of Tiny Slim Crachett, a genuine reprobate
Who squandered his money and wasted his love until it was almost too late.
He was just your typical cowboy; honest, brave and sincere
And he lay on his bunk one Christmas Eve night belching up nachos and beer

When a vision appeared at the foot of his bed. He stared at the apparition,
"Must be that microwave pizza I ate," He blinked and shifted position.
"I ain't no pizza you commonbred fool! Your brain's as dull as your knife!
I am the ghost of Christmas Eve past and Cowboy . . . This is your life!!!"

The scruffy old ghost looked down at the cowboy, *"I'm here for a couple of things;*
To find some reason to salvage your soul and, in doing so, earn me my wings.
I've jotted some notes from the big tally book regarding your skipping on bail.
It says that your mother posted the bond. Is it true that she went to jail?"

"Well," said the cowboy, "It was just for a year. I had to move in with my aunt!
But I got her a job when she made parole pullin' hides at the renderin' plant."
"Yer worse than I thought! It's a hopeless case, and me with my wings on the line!
I've checked through yer records for somethin' worthwhile. There's really not much I can find.

"You rattle around in your sister's ol' truck with no visible means of support.
If sorry and worthless came bottled in pints you'd be good for a quart!
You gypo some cows and ride a few colts, do day work if all else fails,
Shoot pool and drink beer, rope three days a week, trade chronics at all of the sales.

"Your past is a trip through the cat box of life, a sordid collection of wrecks!
You've broke enough hearts to frighten DeBakey and written so many bad checks
Were they laid on the ground in a line end to end they'd reach further than you could point!
Though time is a teacher, you've failed the grade. I can't see a thing that you've loint!

"But, what the heck, it's Christmas, a time of goodwill so I'm willin' to skip the above
If we can find a single good deed you've done that shows kindness and love."
"Humm . . . kindness and love . . . ?" thought Tiny Slim Crachett, his mind beginning to race,
"Once a rumor got started that Mother's old farm was covered with toxic waste!

"For the sake of my mom, I rallied the press. To a man they took up her cause!
Greenpeace rowed up and camped on the lawn, the feminists all burned their bras!
"I handcuffed myself to the Fridgidaire! And went on a hunger strike!
But alas we failed. She was forced to sell at less than I would have liked.

"Thank goodness I'd just got my real estate license 'cause the place brought near '43'
Though it cost the 'ol lady twenty-two thou for commission and realtor's fee.
"So there's my good deed. As simple as that. You can count on me in a pinch.
Our problem is solved, I'm home free and clear and your wings are a lead pipe cinch!

"So, let's drink a toast to Mom and the angels, and you, though you're a late bloomer,
And hope they never find out it was me who started that ugly rumor!"

152

The First Cowboy's Fall From Grace

To those of you who've wondered why the cowboy's life is hard,
   Why misfortune seems to track him with utter disregard
For his proud and noble calling, from which he's never strayed,
   My friends, I'm here to tell ya why it rains on his parade!

Go back to the beginning when the earth was fresh and new,
   When there were no cattle buyers and never interest due.
The BLM just had one truck and no allotments leased,
   The grass was green and belly deep, untouched by man or beast.

God scrutinized the open range, unsatisfied, somehow. . .
   "What's the point of all this grass if we ain't got a cow?"
He took some mud from Pincher Creek, an egg from Cedarville,
   Hyannis horns and Dalhart hair and squeezin's from a still,

He breathed the north wind in her lungs and gave her tail a twist
   And thus was born the first four leg-ged horticulturist.
They multiplied like rabbits and they covered all the land.
   From north to south they ran amok! 'Til things got out of hand!

God gave the problem lots of thought and soon the answer came
   "I think I'll build a cowboy 'cause we need someone to blame!"
He gathered raw materials from what He had at hand
   Then mixed'em on the river bank with gravel, bark and sand.

He scooped the cowboy from the clay and forged him in the fire
   "I'm leavin' you to run these cows without a rope or wire
They'll give you meat and milk and love and never stray from sight
They'll keep you for eternity if you just treat 'em right

"But there may be temptations and if your conscience drifts
    I warn you now to just beware of coyotes bearing gifts."
For quite awhile he towed the line and great was his reward
    But soon all this prosperity begat the cowboy bored.

He got to hangin' out at night with ropers and their ilk.
    He started tradin' green broke colts and drinkin' tiger milk!
Then late one night in Rocky Ford while he was shootin' pool
    The coyote racked 'em up and said, *"I see you ain't no fool.*

"Yer cows are makin' you a bunch, yer in the catbird seat.
    Yer only lackin' just one thing to make yer life complete . . . "
"Git thee behind me, Coyote! I'm forewarned about thy sting!"
    The coyote grinned his evil grin, said, *"Have a chicken wing!"*

He knew he shouldn't do it but he tried a little piece,
    "Say, this ain't really all that bad. . . it needs a bit of grease,
Here, let me taste that drumstick, there, this really satisfies."
    He stuffed himself with chicken breasts, with gizzards, hearts and thighs,

He lost all track of time and place and ate 'til he exclaimed
    "I've tasted the forbidden fruit and now I am ashamed!"
God found him in the horse barn with fried chicken on his breath
    "I see you've lost your innocence. . . Your fate is worse than death!

"I told you, shun the coyote but you've disobeyed my trust
    Now you're condemned to ride the drag, forever eatin' dust!"
The land dried up, his cows got thin, the wind commenced to blow.
    The market never went his way, he always sold'em low.

156

The Forest Service badgered him and moved him every week.
    His blue-eyed heeler bitch got settled by the neighbor's Peke(ingese).
His sheep still made him money though it wasn't quite enough
    But when the wetback left, he knew that things were gettin' tough!

Until, at last, he found himself in town on sale day
    Expounding to a stranger who had chanced to pass his way,
"Once I ran cows in Paradise! My strays were never out
    Horn flies were non-existent then, we'd never heard of drought,

"But then I fell a victim to temptation's sly deceit . . .
    I've paid the price in hemorrhoids and blisters on my seat!
The horse the coyote gave me is the only one I've got
    But ridin' him is murder 'cause he never breaks a trot!

"I'm down to drinkin' goat's milk now, to keep my ulcer calm
    And parts of me are plum wore out and ready to embalm!
I'm doomed to spend forever at the back end of a cow.
    If I'd never tasted chicken. . . I'd be an angel now."

With that the cowboy drained his glass and stared out into space
    A victim of his own thin grit, that let him fall from grace.
But his spirit was undaunted in spite of his distress
    As witnessed by his comments when he added this P.S.,

"But I'm not one to give up hope. It's not the cowboy way.
    If this drought'll end tomorrow, I think I'll be okay
And my luck jist might be changin' if I can just maintain
    'Cause the coyote talked to Noah. . . *he* thinks it's gonna rain!"

AARP!

Of late there's been a modest debate
involving the wearing of fur.
There's some even swears anybody who wears it
is flawed in their character.
Yet others will fight to maintain their right
to wear what they dang well please
But the answer lies in a compromise
that sets both minds at ease.

Imagine two friends at opposite ends
who meet and do lunch once a week.
Their friendship is tried when they gather outside
a Beverly Hills boutique,
"Sylvia, oh my soul, is that a mink stole?
Please tell me it's fake from Goodwill!"
*"Yes, Babs, it is mink, but it's not what you think,
because...it's designer roadkill!"*

Oh, sure, you scoff, but don't blow it off
it's the wisdom of Solomon's voice.
The perfect solution, it grants absolution
yet leaves the owner Pro Choice!
Wisdom so pure should forever endure
and percolate into your soul
So I'm the head jack of the Animal Ac-
cident Recovery Patrol!

The AARP! Which is Larry and me,
are on the road every night
To gently remind you that mess left behind you
is more than a buzzard's delight!
Carry your trowel for mammal or fowl
to collect your vehicular blooper.
In time you will find yucky's all in your mind,
no worse than a pooper scooper!

Plus, you'll be amazed how activists praise you
for doin' what you think is right
And no trapper'd object if you stopped to collect
things that go bump in the night.
But treat it with care, waste not a hare,
be sorry, but don't sit and pine,
'Cause accidents happen when yer both overlappin'
the double yellow line.

So salvage your plunder and render your blunder
into a warm winter coat
And remember our motto as you know you otto
it follows, and herein I quote,
"MAKE IT A HABIT TO PICK UP YOUR RABBIT
DON'T LEAVE HIM TO DRY IN THE SUN
FOR THE SAKE OF A GARMENT, RECYCLE YOUR VARMINT
IT'S TACKY TO JUST HIT AND RUN!"

ANONYMOUS END

I'm here at an old pal's funeral
    Not too many people have come
Just a few of us boys from the outfit
    So he don't go out like a bum.

Seems like I've known him forever
    As I look back over the years
We've rode several wagons together
    And shared a couple of beers.

He never quite made it to foreman
    But then, of course, neither have I.
He always sorta stayed to the center
    Just kind of a regular guy.

He'd always chip in for a party
    Though he was never one to get loud.
Everything that he did was just average
    He never stood out in a crowd.

He was fair with a rope and a rifle,
    He was never early or late.
In the pickup he rode in the middle
    So he'd never open a gate.

Conversin' with him was plum easy
    He never had too much to say,
No matter what question you'd ask him
    The answer was always, "Okay."

Well, they've lowered him down to the hard pan
    And we've sung 'Shall we gather at'
They've asked for a moment of silence
    And everyone's holdin' their hat.

Now the preacher is askin' me kindly
    To say a few words at his death
So I mumble, and say, "He was steady. . ."
    Then I pause and take a deep breath

But I'm too choked up to continue.
    The crowd thinks I've been overcame
But the mason has screwed up his tombstone
    And I can't remember his name!

THE FLAG

Ladies and gentlemen, I give you the flag
That flew over Valley Forge
Was torn in two by the gray and the blue
And bled through two world wars.

I give you the flag that burned in the street
In protest, in anger and shame,
The very same flag that covered the men
Who died defending her name.

We now stand together, Americans all,
Either by choice or by birth
To honor the flag that's flown on the moon
And changed the face of the earth.

History will show this flag stood a friend
To the hungry, the homeless and lost
That a mixture of men as common as clay
Valued one thing beyond cost.

And they've signed it in blood from Bunker Hill
To Saigon, Kuwait and Toko Ri.
I give you the flag that says to the world
Each man has a right to be free.

RALPH'S TREE

Ralph planted the tree next to the house so it would get run-off from the roof. He put it outside the bathroom window so he and Mary could see it often. As the years slid by Ralph gave it special care. It was strange to see a grizzled old rancher fondly tending his tree. But it grew, which was no small accomplishment in the sun baked prairie of eastern Montana. It withstood the blizzards and dry spells, the searing wind and meager soil, just like the people who inhabit that hard country.

The tree didn't exactly flourish but it lived and grew. It was a symbol. It marked a spot of civilization in an unforgiving land. Ralph rested easier knowing the tree grew in his yard. It gave Mary comfort.

Birds came and nested in it. It stood as tall as it could and did its best to repay Ralph's attention by shading a little more of the house every year. Although Ralph would probably never say it, I figger he loved that tree.

I can understand. I've spent my life planting trees. Wherever I've lived trees were not plentiful. . . the Panhandle of Texas, southern New Mexico, the California desert, the sagebrush country of Idaho and the plains of Colorado. I'd move into a place and plant a few trees. I had to lay pretty flat to get any shade. Then I'd move on before I could hang a hammock. Yup, I know how Ralph felt about his tree.

The Empire Builder, Amtrak's Pride of the North, runs from Chicago to Spokane. It comes through Ralph's country. Eastern Montana was dry as a Death Valley dirt road that summer of '88. Sparks from the train started a range fire. The wall of flame was 30 feet high and moving 40 mph when Ralph smelled the smoke. He and Mary escaped with their lives and little else. The house, the outbuildings, the machinery and the garden were burned to the ground. They'd been on the ranch 58 years. Fifty-eight years.

They're staying in town now. Their lawyer is working on a settlement with the railroad. It'll take time. Something Ralph doesn't want to waste. He's 81.

Ralph's tree is a stick. As dead as a steel post. As dead as a dream.

Ralph, my heart goes out to you, sir. But I know as sure as the sun comes up tomorrow, you have to plant another tree. . . and soon.

Then this winter you can look forward to spring when that little tree will leaf out and start casting a shadow on the ashes of your pain.

RANGE FIRE

Lightning cracked across the sky like veins on the back of your hand.
It reached a fiery finger out as if in reprimand
And torched a crippled cottonwood that leaned against the sky
While grass and sagebrush hunkered down that hellish hot July.

The cottonwood exploded! And shot its flaming seeds
Like comets into kerosene, igniting all the weeds.
The air was thick as dog's breath when the fire's feet hit the ground.
It licked its pyrogenic lips and then it looked around.

The prairie lay defenseless in the pathway of the beast.
It seemed to search the further hills and pointed to the east,
Then charged! Like some blind arsonist, some heathen hell on wheels
With its felonious companion, the wind, hot on his heels.

The varmints ran like lemmings in the shadow of the flame
While high above a red tailed hawk flew circles, taking aim.
He spied a frazzled prairie dog and banked into a dive
But the stoker saw him comin' and fried 'em both alive!

It slid across the surface like a molten oil slick.
It ran down prey and predator... the quiet and the quick.
The killdeer couldn't trick it, it was cinders in a flash.
The bones of all who faced it soon lay smoking in the ash.

The antelope and cricket, the rattlesnake and bee,
The butterfly and badger, the coyote and the flea.
It was faster than the rabbit, faster than the fawn,
They danced inside the dragon's mouth like puppets. . . then were gone.

It offered up no quarter and burned for seven days.
A hundred thousand acres were consumed within the blaze.
Brave men came out to kill it, cutting trail after trail
But it jumped their puny firebreaks and scattered 'em like quail.

It was ugly from a distance and uglier up close
So said the men who saw the greasy belly of the ghost.
It made'm cry for mama. Melted tracks on D-8 Cats.
It sucked the sweat right off of their backs and broke their thermostats.

It was hotter than a burning brake, heavy as a train,
It was louder than the nightmare screams of Abel's brother, Cain.
It was war with nature's fury unleashed upon the land
Uncontrollable, enormous, it held the upper hand.

The men retrenched repeatedly, continuously bested
Then finally on the seventh day, like Genesis, it rested.
The black-faced fire fighters stared, unable to believe.
They watched the little wisps of smoke, mistrusting their reprieve.

They knew they hadn't beaten it. They knew beyond a doubt.
Though *News Break* told it different, they knew it just went out.
Must've tired of devastation, grew jaded to the fame.
Simply bored to death of holocaust and walked out of the game.

You can tell yourself...*that's crazy.* Fire's not a living thing.
It's only chance combustion, there's no malice in the sting.
You can go to sleep unworried, knowing man is in control,
That these little freaks of nature have no evil in their soul.

But rest assured it's out there and the powder's always primed
And it will be back, you know it...it's only biding time
'Til the range turns into kindling and the grass turns into thatch
And a fallen angel tosses out a solitary match.

THE TWENTY-DOLLAR ROPE

Tom says it oughta be against the law to sell a rope for $20. It's like buyin' two white mice for yer kid. They're so cute that first day in their little cage. A five-pound bag of Purina Rodent Chow looks like it'll last forever. By the time you're orderin' 20 tons of Rodent Grower Mix in the bulk, it's too late to call the cat!

Roping starts off innocent enough. Get the feel of it. Maybe buy a dummy head for $18.95 to stick in a haybale in the backyard. Then Leo Camarillo's book for $9.95 and a 98-cent pair of roping gloves. Just a way to kill time, you say.

Without meaning to, you start hangin' around team ropers. Talk centers around roping. It eventually gets around to horses. Your horse has about as much interest in roping as your wife does! Somebody mentions a good rope horse for sale. Maybe you oughta go look. Only $1,800. No more than a family season ski pass. The kids can go next year.

You start reading the *Roper Sports News* and the *Western Horseman*. The saddle you've got is serviceable, but if you expect to win, you need one that is built for ropers. You could order a custom built, of course, but that's too expensive and takes too long to get. You compromise and buy one off the rack for $1,100. All you have to cancel is the anniversary trip to Mexico you'd planned with yer wife.

The local jackpot arena is only eight miles from home. Really too far to ride a'horseback twice a week, so you scan the want ads: GOOD USED TWO-HORSE TRAILER -$3,500. Needs a little paint, wiring, license and new tires; another $1,750. Not much more than yer oldest kid's college tuition. She can get a job. Builds character.

You pull yer new horse trailer to the local ropings in yer four-door Chevette. That lasts about six weeks. A new four-wheel drive dualey pick-up, repainted to match the trailer: $18,000. Only have to cash in two C.D.s and take Mother out of the retirement home. Besides, now you can go to some of the ropin's with the toughs. There's a chance to win some real money.

Sunday night, 11:00 p.m., yer wife looks up from her pillow and dutifully asks, "Well, dear, how was the roping today?"

"Almost got third money. Dang loop slipped off one hock. Anyway. I only lost $45."

JUNIOR

Now, Junior is tough and can't git enough
 of lively confrontations
And bein' his friend, I'm asked to defend
 his slight miscalculations.

  Among his mistakes, too often he makes
   none of his business . . . his.
  So I counsel restraint 'cause sometimes he ain't
   as tough as he *thinks* he is!

Like the time he cut loose in a bar called the Moose
 in Dillon on rodeo night.
I stayed on his tail in hopes to prevail
 and maybe prevent us a fight

  But Junior's headstrong and it didn't take long
   'til he got in a debate
  Involving a chair and big hunks of hair
   and startin' to obligate

His friends, I could see, which only was me!
 A fact I couldn't ignore,
So takin' his arm to lead him from harm
 I drug my pal to the door.

  No one disagreed and I thought that we'd
   made our escape free and clear
  But he turned to the crowd and said good and loud,
   "Who is the toughest guy here!"

Not the smartest remark in a place this dark,
 ol' Junior had gone too far!
No one said a word but I knew they heard
 'cause all heads turned to the bar

  And there in the hole like a power pole
   stood the pressure for all his peers.
  "Ugly for Hire" and he wore a truck tire
   that came down over his ears!

He had on some chaps with big rubber straps
 but over his arms instead!
And sported a pattern like the planet Saturn
 his eyebrows went clear round his head!

His good eye glared while his nostrils flared
      like a winded Lippizan
Which lent him the air of a wounded bear
      whose pointer'd been stepped upon!

A Crescent wrench swung from where it hung
   on a log chain wrapped round his neck,
Along with a claw, a circular saw
   and parts from a Harley wreck!

      With his Sumo girt he needed no shirt.
        Hell, he had no place to tuck it!
      And wonders don't cease, he wore a codpiece
        made from a backhoe bucket!

He was Fantasyland, the Marlboro Man
   and heartburn all rolled into one!
From where I was lookin' our goose was cookin',
   our cowboy days were done!

      Then he spoke from the hole like a thunder roll
        that came from under the sea.
      He swallered his snuff. . . said, **"If yer huntin' tough,**
        I reckon that'ud be me."

I heard a pin drop. The clock even stopped!
   Silence...'cept for me heavin'.
But Junior, instead, just pointed and said,
   "You! Take over, we're leavin'!"

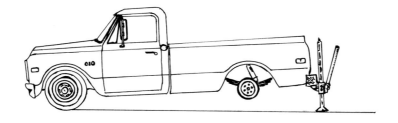

SERIOUS ROPIN'

If yer a sorry roper, friend, let me commiserate
And pass along some wisdom that may help to set you straight.

The reason that yer just no good and why you've never won
Is...You've got the false impression that ropin' should be fun!

Don't kid yourself. It's just like golf. We're talkin' sacrifice!
To rope and win consistently you have to pay the price.

Eliminate the little things that busy up yer life,
Those bothersome distractions like house payments and a wife.

Quit yer job! Forsake the kids! Sell everything you own
And buy a dually gooseneck so you'll never be alone.

Then enter every jackpot where the fools'll take yer check
And practice 'til yer ropin' dummy's got a crooked neck!

Survive on beer and road food. Never falter, never fail
'Cause fingers will grow back, ya know, just like a lizard's tail.

Keep ropin' 'til yer spoken word degenerates to grunts
Or simply, *"I'm a heela...but sometimes I wope the fwonts."*

And maybe you might beat the odds but be prepared because
Each dally man will have to face the roper's mentalpause.

Eventually the time will come when nothin' reconciles.
You'll be burnt out from front to back with cavities and piles,

Yer rope won't reach out like it did, yer loop just won't quite fit.
You can't remember if yer can is filled with beer or spit!

There's only one place left to go, so muster yer resources,
Change yer name and get a loan, start trainin' cuttin' horses!

HEADER OR HEELER

If you saw a team roper with his hands behind his back, could you tell if he was a header or a heeler? I have done an extensive study on this very problem with a grant funded equally by the Pro Rodeo Ex-Wives Collection Agency and the TRA (Team Ropers Anonymous) Halfway House. Here are the results of my findings:

Headers are more likely to have their hair styled rather than cut. Heelers get their hair cut bi-annually and usually need a shave.

A header owns a fairly new truck and trailer with a coordinated paint job. A heeler buys recaps and the paint job on his trailer matches the primer on his brother-in-law's barbecue grill.

A header will often have two horses, his favorite and one in training. A heeler will have one horse - in training and for sale!

A header may own his own arena. The heeler usually owes last week's stock charge!

The header carefully positions his horse in the box, checks for steer alertness and nods at precisely the moment everything is perfect.

The heeler is jerked awake when the head gate bangs!

The tack box of a header contains an extra set of reins, leather punch, fly spray, snaps, saddle blanket talcum, horn wraps, assorted brushes and combs, a second tie down, various sizes of leather straps, cotton rolls, leg brace solution, hoof care tools, dikes, two pair each of bell boots and splint boots, a jar of silver polish and a can of assorted brake light bulbs.

A heeler's tack box will have a warm bottle of Combiotic, some Bute paste, an inner tube, a hatchet, some 14-gauge wire, a nest of baler twine, an 18-piece Taiwanese socket set, a runnin' iron, beer opener and one skid boot!

The header has ulcers. The heeler has a hangover.

A header will discuss the lineage of his horse, "He's out of an Easy Jet mare and full cousin to Stick."

A heeler will discuss the lineage of his tack, "I used to ride broncs with this saddle. It's an association tree but I bolted on this horn and wrapped it with duct tape and rawhide. Dee Pickett gimme this halter."

A header will blame his horse, himself, his rope, his wrap, his saddle, his timing, his technique, his dally, his loop, the steer, the wind or overtraining.

The heeler blames the header!

FRECKLE'S ADVICE

Though Freckles is an angel now, he ain't forgot his friends.
He drops to earth and hangs around behind the buckin' pens.
He pulls a rope or just makes sure a rider gets bucked free
So I took it as an honor, the day he spoke to me . . .

"I saw you ride your bull today. You sure did yourself proud.
You had him by the short hairs, I could feel it in the crowd!"
"I really should be thankful that I even stayed aboard.
You could'a done it better, Freckles . . . I'm lucky that I scored!"

"Hey don't be puttin' yourself down! You know you did okay.
The time will come when you'll look back and hunger for today
When everything was workin' right and judges liked your style,
Your joints were smooth, your belly flat and girls liked your smile.

'Cause in between the best you rode and the last one that you'll try
You'll face your own mortality and look it in the eye.
There ain't no shame admittin' you ain't what you used to be,
The shame is blamin' Lady Luck when Father Time's the key!

So if they know you came to ride and always did your best
Then hang your ol' spurs up with pride, 'cause that's the acid test
And, say some gunsel offers you a 'Geritol on Ice,'
Just grin 'im down, 'cause you don't have to ride Tornado twice!"

RODEO MOM

His mother was glad he wasn't hurt worse.
  As it was he went out on a stretcher.
She sat in the stands and swallowed a curse
  Holding her heart and trying to catch'er

    Breath that was sucked from her very being.
      She rose like a wraith, guided by loving
    Eyes wide open but not really seeing.
      Floating, she thought, but pushing and shoving

To get to his side as others gave way.
  Close calls flashed through her mind as she hurried,
He'd always survived but each night she'd pray
  Seeking an ally. God knew she worried.

    Dreams. Horns as heavy as railroad ties,
      Battleship hooves that smoked and tore black holes
    In the flesh of her babies. Terrorized
      She'd wake, shaking until she gained control.

She'd signed permission in his younger years.
  "NOTE: WE TAKE NO RESPONSIBILITY".
Signed it. Released him into atmospheres
  Uncharted. Knowing his mortality.

    She hasn't had to sign for quite a while
      She thinks as she reaches the ambulance.
    He's grown. She takes his hand and tries to smile
      And reminds herself this is what he wants.

He squeezes her hand and grins sheepishly.
  "Sign this form," the driver is declaring.
Once more she signs her name. An irony
  That spares not the mothers of the daring.

CASEY COME CALLIN'

The devil stood by at the gates of Hell
        Watchin' the sinners in line
When Casey drove up in a Cadillac
        Purple as Thunderbird wine,

"Hey, boy! You with yer tail in the dirt!
        How about parkin' my car!
I aim to have a look around. If ya
        Need me, I'll be in the bar!"

The devil choked...*"Don't you know who I am!"*
        "Can't say as I place ya, Bud?
But just from the look of them puny horns
        Yer packin' some Jersey blood!"

The devil caught up with Case in the lounge
        Chargin' his drinks on the house
A rope in one hand and wrapped 'round his neck,
        A piece of a lady's blouse!

He was tellin' tall tales of rodeo days!
        The crowd was havin' a ball
'Cause after each round he'd bang on the bar
        And smash his glass on the wall!

The devil was...peeved! *"Just look at this mess!*
        You raised with a buffalo?"
Casey glanced round the room, *"This dump looks just right,*
        This here ain't Maxim's, ya know!

I reckon it's time that we checked your stock,"
        He jerked on the devil's tail,
"Contractors like you most always have junk
        To poison a buckin' horse sale!"

Well, he rode'm all! Some two or three times!
        All at the devil's expense
And just for a lark he jerked a few steers
        And tore out a mile of fence!

Then he jumped aboard the devil's best bronc
    And kicked him into a trot.
They shot out the gate like snoose through a goose
    And straight to the parkin' lot

Where the devils had built a flea market
    For sellin' their second best.
He roped the pole of the tent on the end
    And drug it plum through the rest!

He'z goin' flat out when he crossed the grass
    Of the only lawn in Hell.
The devil's wife screamed when he tipped his hat
    And bid her a fond farewell!

He rode through her house and out the back door
    Draggin' curtains and carpet behind,
No dish was untouched, no dog was uncussed,
    No car on the street was aligned

When Casey got through! Apocalypse reigned!
    Everything razed to the ground!
The devil was desperate when he caught up
    And flagged the cowboy down.

"Here's the keys to yer car! I've gassed it up,
    Yer back's all I wanna see!
You showed up too soon, we ain't ready for you
    And son, we may never be!

If you can't tell, Hell's a bad enough place
    Without you makin' it worse.
So do me a favor when your time comes . . .
    Try the other place first."

POO BAH

I BELIEVE HE SAW ME COMIN'
HORSE TRADERS USUALLY DO!
"I've got this chestnut gelding,
Might be just the horse for you.

Two trainers from Kentucky
Plan to look at him today.
I really shouldn't show him
But first come, first serve, I say.

He's the best I've got to offer,
None better anywhere,"
THEN HE SAW ME EYE THE FILLY.
"Except, of course, that mare.

She's raced a million dirt tracks,
Everyone where I'm not barred."
I RAISED A CROOKED EYEBROW.
"Though, I never ran her hard.

She's as sound as Rockerfeller,
As healthy as ol' Shep,"
I FELT THE SCARS WHERE SHE'D BEEN NERVED.
"Precautionary step."

I RAN MY FINGERS DOWN HER LEG.
HER HOCKS WERE BIG AND SOFT.
"Mosquito bites, I reckon,
I'll throw in a can of Off."

SHE COUGHED AND RAISED A HEAVE LINE
THAT WOULD SCARE AN AUCTIONEER.
"The pollen count's been high this week,
Hay fever's bad this year.

I've priced her at a thousand bucks.
A bargain any day
"But I'd consider half that much
If you took her today."

AS I STARTED FOR THE PICKUP
HE PLAYED HIS FINAL ACE,
"She's bred to Poo Bah's brother's son,
The finest stud to race."

I HELD MY NOSE TO SHOW HIM
POO BAH WASN'T DIDDLY SQUAT.
HE BLINKED AND QUICKLY ADDED,
"But I don't believe she caught!"

RUNNIN' WILD HORSES

The chase, the chase, the race is on
  The mustangs in the lead
    The cowboys hot behind the band
      Like centaurs, blurred with speed
        The horses' necks are ringin' wet
          From keepin' up the pace
            And tears cut tracks into the dust
              Upon the rider's face
The rank ol' mare sniffs out the trail
  While never breakin' stride
    But fast behind the wranglers come
      Relentless, on they ride
        Until the canyon walls close in
          And punch'em through the gap
            Where bottled up, they paw and watch
              The cowboy shut the trap
And that's the way it's been out west
  Since Cortez turned'em loose
    We thinned the dinks and with the herd
      We kept an easy truce
        But someone said they'd all die off
          If cowboys had their way
            So they outlawed runnin' horses
              But who am I to say
'Cause, hell, I'm gettin' older, boys
  And though I miss the chase
    His time, like mine, has come and gone
      We're both so out of place
        The glamour of our way of life
          Belies our common fate
            I'm livin' off my pension check
              And he's a ward of state
But what a time! When he and I
  Ran hard across the land
    Me breathin' heavy down his neck
      Him wearin' no man's brand
        No papers gave us ownership
          To all the ground we trod
            But it belonged to me and him
              As sure as there's a God
And if I could, I'd wish for him
  And for myself, likewise
    To finally cross the Great Divide
      Away from pryin' eyes
        So in the end he has a chance
          To die with dignity
            His carcass laid to rest out there
              Where livin', he ran free
And coyotes chew his moldered bones
  A fitting epilogue
    Instead of smashed up in a can
      For someone's townhouse dog.

The BUCKSKIN MARE

illustrated by Dave Holl

"A story not unlike *THE BUCKSKIN MARE* was passed down as true, although the characters and location were of my choosing. A cowboy became obsessed with capturing an elusive wild horse. Unable to rope her, in his madness and frustration, he shot her. He was ostracized by his fellow cowboys and drifted off.

Strangely enough, had he captured her 'fair and square', brought her in and shot her on Main Street, his story would have ended differently.

His crime, which concerned itself less with legal text and more with 'doin' the right thing' is as real today as it was then. It's all part of the *Code of the West*."

baxter

*H*e was every burnt out cowboy
that I'd seen a million times

With dead man penny eyes,
like tarnished brass,

That reflected accusations
of his critics and his crimes

And drowned them
in the bottom of a glass.

"*H*e's a victim," said the barkeep,
"Of a tragic circumstance.

Down deep inside him,
bad luck broke an egg.

Now his longtime compañeros
and his sagebrush confidants

All treat him like a man
who's got the plague."

*H*e was damn sure death warmed over,
human dust upon the shelf,

Though Grasmere ain't
the center of the earth

He appeared like he'd be lonesome
at a party for himself,

So low was his opinion
of his worth.

"*P*our me two, and make'm doubles."
Then I slid on down the bar

And rested at the
corner of his cage.

I had judged him nearly sixty
when I saw him from afar

But eye to eye,
I'd overshot his age.

'Cause it wasn't time that changed him,
I could see that now up close,

Pure hell had cut
those tracks across his face.

His shaking hand picked up the drink,
then he gestured grandiose,

"This buys you
chapter one of my disgrace.

It was twenty years, September,
that I first laid eyes on her,

Not far from where
this story's bein' told.

She was pretty, in an awkward way,
though most would not concur,

A buckskin filly,
comin' two years old.

We were runnin' wild horses
on the Blackstone range that day.

We found'em on the flats
right after dawn.

There was me and Tom and Ziggy,
plus some guys from Diamond A.

They caught our scent
and then the race was on!

We hit'em like a hurricane
and we pressed'em to the east

A'crowdin'em
against the canyon rim

'Til the fear of God was boilin'
in the belly of the beast

And chance of their escape
was lookin' dim.

We all held the bunch together
and we matched'em stride for stride.

I took the flank
so none of them would stray.

Then I saw that buckskin filly
take a trail down the side,

I rode on by
and let her get away.

'No big deal,' I told my cronies,
as we later reminisced

And celebrated
with a glass of beer,

'She would'a made poor chicken feed,
so I'm sorta glad I missed.

I'll get her when we
crack'em out next year.

Shor'enuf, next fall we found'em
up on California Crick.

The buckskin mare
was still amongst the pack.

I had made a little wager
and I aimed to make it stick,

Whoever roped her
pocketed the jack.

We lined'em out and built our loops.
Then ignoring protocol,

That mare changed course
and never missed a beat!

She took dang near the entire bunch
when she climbed the canyon wall

And left us empty handed
at her feet.

*In the several years that followed
she eluded each attempt*

*To capture her, in fact,
she seemed amused*

*And her reputation deepened,
as no doubt, did her contempt*

*For us, the bumbling cowboys
she abused.*

*The legend of the buckskin mare,
which to me, was overblown,*

*Was bunkhouse, barroom
gossip everywhere.*

*She achieved a kinda stature,
way beyond mere flesh and bone,*

*And stories of her deeds
would raise your hair.*

*Some attributed her prowess
to a freak in Nature's Law.*

*Still others said
she was the devil's spawn*

*So the incident that happened
at the top of Sheepshead Draw*

*Served notice hell's account
was overdrawn.*

*'Cause upon that fateful gather
there was one foolhardy dope,*

*A greenhorn kid
who didn't have a care*

*But susceptible to eggin'
and right handy with a rope*

*So, 'course, we pumped him up
about the mare.*

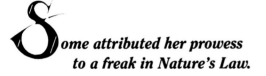

He was lathered up and tickin'
like an ol' two dollar watch

When we spotted
the object of the game.

Though we wanted other horses,
each one ached to carve his notch

On the buckskin mare,
Bruneau Canyon's fame.

They were down amongst the willers
by a muddy water hole.

The kid went first.
He had her in his sights

And halfway up the other side
where the slick rock takes its toll

He caught that buckskin legend
dead to rights!

He was screamin' bloody murder
as she clawed her way uphill!

He pitched the slack
and pulled his horse up hard!

She was jerked around and faced the kid,
and friend, if looks could kill

I'd have folded before
she played her card.

But the kid began descending
with his back turned toward the mare

He planned to choke her down,
I won't deny,

But she jumped from high above him,
like a bird takes to the air,

She looked for all the world
like she could fly.

*T*ime was frozen for an instant
as she leaped out into space,

A piece from some unholy carousel

And I stared, slack jawed and helpless,
in the morbid scene's embrace,

Oddly peaceful,
until the hammer fell.

*S*he came down like fallin' timber!
Like a screamin' mortar shell

And scattered terra firma
in her wake!

She lit runnin' off his wrong side
like a thoroughbred gazelle!

That nylon rope was hissin'
like a snake!

*I*t flipped behind the kid's own horse.
Laid the trip as sweet as pie.

She thundered by him
takin' up the slack!

The rope drew tight around his hocks,
then she shifted into high

And jerked that horse
right over on his back!

'*C*ourse the kid fell backwards with him.
In my heart I knew his fate.

His soul was headed
for the great beyond.

She was draggin' horse and rider
like a bundle of deadweight

When Clay rode in
and cut the fatal bond.

*S*he escaped. That goes unspoken,
toward the seeding to the west.

To our dismay
the kid had breathed his last.

She had spread his brains all over,
but ol' Maxie said it best,

'That's what ya get
fer tyin' hard and fast.'

The years creaked by like achin' joints.
Driftin' cowboys came and went.

The buckskin mare,
she held her own and stayed.

She became a constant rumor
and engendered discontent

Among the bucks
whose reps had not been made.

But to me she was an omen.
Like a black cat on the prowl.

I had no admiration
for her kind.

She began to stalk my nightmares,
an obsession loud and foul

Only drinkin'
would get her off my mind.

There were still a few ol' timers
like Jess and Dale, Chuck and Al,

Who spoke of her
as one without a fault.

They bragged her up,
which didn't do a thing for my morale

'Cause I'd begun to dread
each new assault.

But I went, like I did always,
when they organized last year.

We met at Simplot's
Sheep Crick winter camp

Then headed east toward J P Point,
it was sunny, warm and clear

But I was cold.
My bones were feelin' damp.

*I*t was gettin' close to lunch time
when we finally cut their track

And found'em at the
Bruneau Canyon's verge.

We rode in like mad Apaches!
I was leadin' the attack!

The first to see us comin'
was the scourge.

*T*he scourge of all my sleepless nights.
The bogeyman in my dreams.

I told myself,
this run would be her last.

She ducked across my horse's nose,
to draw me out, it seems.

I followed suit and
then the die was cast.

*S*he went straight for Bruneau Canyon,
made a B-line for the edge.

My head was ringin'
with her siren's song

Then she hesitated briefly,
sorta hung there on the ledge

Like she was darin' me
to come along.

*T*hen she wheeled, without a 'by yer leave'
and disappeared from view.

I reached the precipice
and never slowed!

I could hear the boys shoutin'
but by then I think they knew

I was rabid
and ready to explode!

We landed like an avalanche,
my horse, a livin' landslide!

I'll never know
just how he kept his feet.

My boot hooked on a buckbrush limb
and whipped me like a riptide,

And in the crash,
I damn near lost my seat!

But I kept the spurs dug in him
as I held the mare in sight.

Varmints skittered,
as down the side we tore!

There were boulders big as boxcars,
Rocks who'd never lost a fight,

That stepped aside
to watch this private war.

Then the cunning crowbait got me!
She came up to this ravine

And jumped it!
Looked to me like just for show.

But I reined up hard and halted.
There was twenty feet between

My horse's hooves
and sure death down below.

But no horse, no fleabag mustang,
was a match for my resolve.

I drove the steel
in my pony's hide

'Til he leaped above the chasm!
I could feel his fear dissolve

As we sailed, soaring,
flaunting suicide!

An eternity of seconds
that concluded in a wreck

The likes of which
you've never seen before.

Nearly cleared the far embankment,
got his front feet on the deck

And pawed like someone
swimmin' for the shore!

Then he shook one final shudder
and went limp between my knees.

I scrambled off him,
prayin' not to fall.

He'd impaled himself upon a rock
and died without a wheeze,

His guts a'stringin'
down the crevice wall.

Then his carcass started saggin',
slippin' off the bloody skewer.

I lunged to save my rifle
from the slide!

My revenge was all that mattered,
a disease that had no cure

Save the stretchin'
of one ol' buckskin's hide.

I stood up and tried to spot her
but my head was feelin' light,

I knew she might be
hidin' anyplace.

Then I heard some pebbles clatter
up above and to my right

And there she waited . . .
laughing in my face.

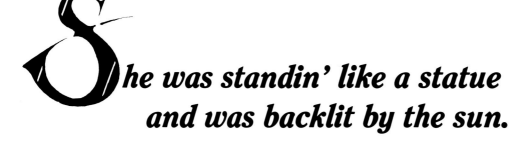

She was standin' like a statue
and was backlit by the sun.

I shook so hard
coins rattled in my jeans.

I could feel my heartbeat poundin'
like the recoil of a gun.

My rowels were janglin'
tunes like tambourines.

As I raised the shakin' rifle,
bugs were crawlin' in my veins.

I levered in a shell
for her demise.

A thirty-thirty center fire,
one hundred and fifty grains,

And shot'er dead . . .
right between the eyes.

You could hear that gunshot echo
all the way to Mountain Home.

The rolling boom
just seemed to stay and stay

And it drummed its disapproval
like a dying metronome,

A requiem
that haunts me to this day.

I climbed out of Bruneau Canyon
with my saddle and my gear.

A grizzly greeting
filled me with despair.

See, my so-called friends left me to rot.
The reason why, was clear,

They'd staked a cross . . .
in honor of the mare.

The rest, well, you can figger out.
But my daddy always said,

'You gotta play the hand
that you been dealt.'

I done made that sow a martyr
and I wish that I was dead,

Because, my friend,
I know how Judas felt.''

About the Artists . . .

BOB BLACK - Bob was first reported in 1946 by a group of wall-eyed insomniacs bivouaced at the foot of an old cow in Idaho. Officially labeled a hoax by the Air Force, who lost over seven cases of whiskey in a dramatic pursuit, Bob soon proved real enough when he stepped forward on national radio to receive the title of "Honorary Weasel" from the Blanche Dunlap School of Beauty.

He quickly became a household word and his trademark outfit; boots, a decrowned Resistol, tarpaper pants and a t-shirt emblazoned with the slogan *"Born to Sleep"* was worn by kids everywhere.

Then tragedy struck. It was discovered his treasure trove of witty quips "Bobisms" were not spontaneous and in fact had been written by his dog, Lupe.

Bob slunk south, replaced by **Mayberry RFD** and is now believed living in Antarctica.

DON GILL - Western artist and cattleman, makes his home in Idaho. After spending a lot of years on cattle ranches, feedlots and in rodeo arenas, Don has many actual experiences that inspire his cartoons.

Don and his wife, Denise, believe keeping busy with family and being involved in community activities is the ticket to a happy and healthy life.

DAVE HOLL - At home in northern Nevada, Dave spends most of his time buckarooin' and drawing pictures. With pen and ink in hand, Dave portrays the drama and the humor of the cowboy culture. It's a pretty good way of life.

200

About the Artists . . .

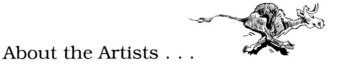

CHARLIE MARSH - Lives on a ranch in Oklahoma with his wife Laurie, two stray dogs and assorted cats.

He does drawings for Farm Journal publications and tries to make a living as a humorous illustrator. He ropes calves on his horse, Mack, for fun and aggravation.

Comments by the Author . . .

Comments: *Friends, I'm proud of this book. Yer in it! All you cowboys, dude wranglers, seed salesmen, harried vets, bankers, bull riders, horse people, broccoli growers, stockdog trainers, trail riders, team ropers, poets, pundits, pole benders, post hole diggers, cattle handlers, chicken haters and lovers of our way of life!*

Cowboy poetry is often funny. I think that stems from the close relationship between humor and tragedy. If you work with livestock you get hurt... A lot! Bit, stepped on, mashed, smashed, bucked off or run over on a regular basis.

If yer in the corral and one of yer amigos gets bucked off, everybody rides over to see if he's alright. If he's alive you start tellin' the story right away! If he's dead, you wait a couple days!

Humor helps you dust yerself off and git back on again.

Thanks for bein' such a great audience and a continuing inspiration.

The End